Smooth Stones & Promises

Fay Rowe

WESTBOW
PRESS
A DIVISION OF THOMAS NELSON

WestBow Press books may be ordered through booksellers or by contacting:

WestBow Press

A Division of Thomas Nelson

1663 Liberty Drive

Bloomington, IN 47403

www.westbowpress.com

1-(866) 928-1240

ISBN: 978-1-4497-3537-1 (sc)

Library of Congress Control Number: 2011963392

Printed in the United States of America

WestBow Press rev. date: 2/16/2012

Also by Fay Rowe

Keepers of the Testimony

25000 Mornings
Ancient Wisdom for a Modern Life

Smooth Stones & Promises

Acknowledgements

The more time I spend on this earth, the more I am convinced that if we are to be all God meant us to be, we need to have an unshakeable trust in him.

Simply, we need to know his integrity.

Since the release of the first edition of this book, entitled *What's In A Name,* I have heard from many who shared how its message of God's faithfulness helped them rest in God's promises.

The purpose of this revised edition is to make the message of God's commitment to his word as accessible as possible. My appreciation goes to those whose input has helped with that goal.

Along with all who inspired, helped, and encouraged me in writing the first edition—Nadine, Diann, Linda, Judi and Glen, Ida, and the London Ready Writers' Group—I want to thank the leaders and members of The Word Guild, a Canadian organization of writers and editors who are Christian. Their annual conference and the membership list-serve support have provided the information and motivation needed for this project.

To Rev. Lorne Rostotski and Dr. Norrel London for their encouragement and kind words of endorsement for the first edition, my gratitude remains.

And to all the other friends and family for their gentle critiques and insightful suggestions, you have my love always, and for your steadfastness and faith, my greatest appreciation.

Contents

PART ONE:
The Search

CHAPTER ONE

Hidden Treasure: The Magnified Word

"I will worship toward thy holy temple,
and praise thy name for thy loving kindness
and for thy truth: for thou hast magnified thy word above all thy
name." ~ Psalm 138:2

1.

ONE LITTLE PHRASE tucked away in Psalm 138:2 says that God has magnified his word above all his name. Hidden in that somewhat obscure phrase is the smooth stone that defeats giants.

Most of us have met Goliath in one form or another. Self-employed and renegade, he wears different disguises—disease, financial ruin, family crisis—but every one of them has the face of a terrorist. Like Goliath in the Bible story, our tormenter shows up to challenge and mock us. We don't even have to see his face. We watch news of war and economic and physical disasters on television; we comfort friends in crisis; we bury loved ones too soon. From down the street or from the other side of the world we can hear his taunt, "You are helpless."

Sometimes, like all but one of the children of Israel, we're convinced Goliath is right. We want nothing more than to run and hide, but we aren't going anywhere. We're paralyzed, perhaps waiting for a David to show up and take out the troublemaker. Hoping, praying for a David.

But giants aren't the only troublemakers we encounter in life. We also face mountains, towering and black, that stand between where we are and where we need to be. Neither as seriously nor immediately threatening as the giants, mountains are still daunting prospects. The sight of them can make us stomach-and-heart sick.

Sometimes the biggest, most disheartening mountain of all is that we simply can't muster the courage to follow a God-given dream. Scaling the heights is not for ordinary people like us. The safe choice, we think, is to stay right where we are and leave the mountains to mountain climbers.

What I've just described is all too common. Those of us who have walked a few miles on this earth have faced and will face circumstances where our confidence is challenged—not only our confidence in ourselves but also our confidence in God.

We may be embarrassed by our struggle. After all, God said he didn't give us a spirit of fear but here we are, shaking in our shoes. We may even wonder if God is paying attention to what we're going through. I remember praying while perched precariously halfway up one of my life's mountains, "God, you see where I am, don't you?"

Often, even though we may know God is watching with loving concern, we still aren't sure he'll get involved to help us. Maybe we don't want to be presumptuous or we don't want to be disappointed. But while we're singing the old hymn "O God Our Help in Ages Past", we really don't expect any help in the present. We hope for it, but…

It may be that our expectation of God's involvement has been tempered by a large dose of what we call realism, born of troubling experience. Perhaps his promises don't ring true anymore. As a result, we don't really *expect* him to do what he says. I remember hearing a Christian television personality say that the promise in Acts 16:31, "Believe on the Lord Jesus Christ and thou shalt be saved," was "the only promise God guarantees to fulfill."

I was shocked when I heard it. I thought I had heard wrong. Then he said it again, "The only one!"

Is that what we really believe? Do we really suppose that all the other promises are not quite as dependable as that one? If we truly believe that, then somewhere along the way our perception of God's character has been distorted, and that is tragic.

This book is about one of the greatest reasons I know of for faith in the promises of God. This reason for believing is as important as our knowledge of God's power and as precious as our assurance of his love for us. It is crucial to our growth as Christians. Without it, we will never develop a strong faith.

This book is about God's integrity.

Most of us will say, and actually do believe, that we have full confidence in God's character, and therefore his integrity. But then what we really believe in our heart—something we might not even be conscious of—slips out.

I hope this book will help you identify what you really believe about God's character, because what we think about God affects our relationship with him and, therefore, our destiny.

The seed of this book was planted in my heart one night deep in the winter of 2002—years before words found their way to a computer screen—when a preacher asked an intriguing question. Here's the story:

"If Anyone Knows, Please Tell Me"

As I lay there quietly, there it was again—the little annoyance that accompanied my latest giant. Three almost imperceptible, simultaneous little "thunks" broke the silence as new numbers found their place. The innocent-looking digital clock taunted me, daring me to see how much of the night was left. I tried to ignore it but the sinister power of the clock compelled me to look. As my nights went of late, this one was still young.

I was at the end of my first month of chemotherapy. I had thought losing my hair would be the hardest part of the deal—vain creature that I am. But nausea was unquestionably the worst of it, and after that, the anti-nausea drugs. I had a complicated love-hate relationship with the drugs. I loved them because they killed the nausea, but hated them because they stole my sleep. Of course, I had the option of sleeping pills to combat the insomnia, but they had their own disagreeable side effect which gave the gallon of water I had to drink a distinct gun metal aftertaste.

Pick your battles, they say, so from that delightful array of nausea, bladder disease, gun metal flavoring, or insomnia, I picked insomnia. And here I was, wide-eyed at 3 a.m., communing bitterly with a clock.

It looked as if sleep was going to elude me again tonight so instead of lying there meditating on my misery, I inched my way out of bed.

Gingerly, quietly—so as not to disturb my husband—I put a teaching tape on the player by my bed.

It was entitled *Strengthen Yourself in the Lord*. I had listened to it many times since the ordeal began, so I knew it would tell me the story of David and his men returning from battle only to find their wives and children taken captive. Heartbroken, the distraught husbands and fathers cried their eyes out. Then, human nature being what it is, they looked for someone to blame and David was the front running candidate.

Poor David! He was still dealing with that on-going King Saul problem; his fair weather friends, the Philistines, didn't want him around anymore; his own family had been captured; and now this! His closest friends and companions were about to stone him to death—a definite downturn in an already messy situation!

Certainly, David had every reason to be discouraged and even terrified. But you have to love this about him: He refused to quit. As the story goes, he "encouraged himself in the Lord his God" (1 Samuel 30:6).

I needed to do what David did. I needed to remind myself of the Lord's presence and strength in my own life.

That's why I put that particular tape on. It wasn't because I was bored or because misery loves company, although the tape would have helped with either of those since the speaker was entertaining and David's troubles more than rivaled my own. It was because it was going to be a long night and the pit of self-pity was too close for comfort. I needed to find a safer place to spend my time because what misery really wants and needs is hope.

Before long, the preacher's voice began to have a sedating effect and I could sense blissful oblivion or even sweet dreams somewhere in the offing. I was nodding off when, from somewhere outside my half-drowse, I heard Pastor Bill Johnson from Bethel Church in Redding, California, quote the scripture from the beginning of this chapter, Psalm 138:2, saying to his congregation, "God has magnified his word above all his name." Then, as if compelled to be honest, he added this afterthought, "… and I don't even know what that means. If any of you know, please tell me."

My eyes popped open.

How had I missed that before? What an odd request for a preacher to make!

If you don't know, please tell me? I was intrigued.

I knew I had found a truth chaser.

Truth Chasers And Treasure Hunters

I'll be the first to admit that truth chasers can be excruciatingly annoying. In fact, they probably should have a support group just to help them with that annoying part. If such a group existed, I expect its membership would be considerable, because, although truth chasers might appear to be an endangered species, if they all came out of the closet we'd find out they are not all that rare.

We all entered this world as truth chasers. Listen to any little one who has just uttered his or her first word. Pretty soon after that first sweet "Dada" or "Mama," we hear a baby's version of "What's that?" At first the parents don't tire of answering that eternal question, but a couple of years go by, the new question is "Why?", and parents tire quickly. Later still, when school teachers have a schedule to keep and question periods have a time limit, the fledgling truth chaser learns to stop chasing.

To the more cynical observers among us it would appear that life, as early as possible, gathers its forces to teach these two lessons: first, questioning too much, or too often, is in poor taste and downright annoying; and second, the need to know is just for a select few.

For those of us who don't learn quickly enough, the lesson is repeated fairly often. I remember an incident that took place back when I was in my twenties. After a Bible study one night, I asked my pastor why John the Baptist was beheaded in prison whereas Peter was set free. I thought it was a reasonable question. Since knowledge is power, I figured if Peter knew something John didn't, I would like to know what it was. After all, it couldn't hurt to know how to deal with trouble without literally losing one's head!

My pastor had no answer except "It was God's will," and although he was kind and patient in his response I came away with the vague feeling I had done something wrong. I had embarrassed myself, as though I had "ripped my britches"—a wonderful phrase from the days I lived in Texas.

I hesitate to tell this second story of squelched truth-chasing because I'm not proud of it. The incident took place one Sunday, soon after the Bible study episode. We had a guest speaker, a luminary from our denomination's head office, who preached on Hebrews 11:1, "Now faith is the substance of things hoped for, the evidence of things not seen." He was a persuasive speaker and it was a well delivered sermon about how calling to mind what God has done in the past will bolster our expectations of his future blessings.

All true, but as he read his text, he changed it so that it now read "faith is the *result* of the substance of things hoped for."

I was disturbed!

In my youthful arrogance and the contention no doubt born of that, I marched up to the front of the church after the service to ask why he felt he could insert the words "result of" into that verse.

It seemed to me that "the substance" and "the result of the substance" must be two different things, and faith couldn't be both. I asked—as innocently as I could—if he was really talking about how experience builds hope, and if so, weren't there other scriptures he could use, for example Romans 5:5. If not that, then was it perhaps that he was giving us a clearer translation of Hebrews 11:1 based on his knowledge of the original language?

To this day, I think my question was sweeter than his response, which was less than gracious. But then, in retrospect, it may be that my sin was greater than his.

I apologized later. He was, after all, a guest at our church and my pastor's friend, so I realized that an apology was in order, especially since in our earlier conversation I had sort of accused him of insulting the intelligence of the congregation by twisting scripture.

My apology predictably met with the same grace as did my question. I recall something about my not being the first woman to attack him. Luckily, I was sufficiently chagrinned by my earlier behavior that I didn't voice what popped into my head: "I'm sure I won't be the last!" Small victory, but it helped. I felt better—redeemed, somehow, from my earlier transgression by resisting this new temptation.

Not theologically correct, I know. I'm not suggesting good works are redemptive: I'm just telling you how I felt.

The outcome of it all: I learned that even when you're in your twenties questioning is still annoying. As well, it is now considered in poor taste.

Sadly, no matter which of us owned the greater fault that day, I walked away from the encounter wondering if there might actually be a universal truth that I hadn't yet clued into: Some things in the Bible are just not meant to be understood. And with that truth, this law: Don't ask!

Thankfully, I don't think I was fully convinced of either, even though for quite a few years after that—in fact, until the day mentioned in my dedication—I set aside the chase in favor of the fulfilling busyness of family life, career, and church service.

Most of my fellow disciples of Jesus seemed to do the same— or, at least, that's how it looked to me. Our lives were full of fairly worthy occupations—working whatever job was our lot; training, feeding, clothing and chauffeuring children; singing in the choir; teaching Sunday school, engaging in everyday "stuff". Of course, there were church services and Bible studies, but it seemed to me we weren't truth chasers there either. Maybe we were just too tired.

Looking back now, it seems that whenever we gave thought to truth it was from the point of view that we had attained its entirety and all that was needed was that we be motivated to live it.

Maybe we assumed there was no need for further illumination. Or perhaps we obeyed a vaguely perceived unspoken rule that said we shouldn't go looking for any. I can't be sure of what was happening in the lives of my peers or my local church during that time, but what I've described is an accurate reflection of how I was feeling.

Those earlier experiences might be the reason why Bill Johnson's request on that tape, "If you know what the magnified word means, tell me," intrigued me. As he quoted Psalm 138:2, he obviously thought he should be able to understand what that verse was telling him, but didn't.

I realize some might not feel the need to understand what God really did when he magnified his word. They might say it's only important that he did it—like we don't need to know what the electrician did when he wired our house. It's just important that it's done.

That may be acceptable when it comes to house wiring, but when it comes to knowledge of God it simply is not okay. We need to know.

David, who wrote the song where this phrase is found, knew what God had done and it meant something to him. Something important enough to cause spontaneous praise to erupt from his lips! Specifically, he worshiped and praised God for his loving kindness and truth.

What if we knew what David knew? Might it have the same effect on us? What if we could grasp what God did when he magnified his word above all his name? Might we, too, be convinced of God's kindness and truth? And might our praise and worship be just as heartfelt as David's?

Maybe it's worth a question or two.

You have probably guessed by now that even though my youthful experience taught me not to question, I've changed my thinking on that. We should never be afraid to question. Questioning is often necessary because understanding, itself, is crucial. The Bible says so. Matthew 13:19 records a conversation Jesus had with His disciples during which he talked about the subject, "When one hears the word of the kingdom, and understands it not, then cometh the wicked one, and catches away that which was sown in his heart."

Apparently, God's word is less likely to be stolen if it is understood. Understanding is, therefore, very important. Proverbs 4:7 instructs us: "with all thy getting, get understanding."

Understanding will help us in more ways than we may know. In Proverbs 3:13-14 we see that "happy is the man who gets understanding, for the merchandise of it is better than the merchandise of silver and the gain thereof than fine gold."

Not just gold, mind you; fine gold! That appears to give emphasis to a statement which already implies that understanding, even more than gold, will be of immense benefit to one who possesses it—not only because of its beauty, but also because of what it will allow its possessor to accomplish.

That brings us—at last!—to the springboard for this book: Psalm 138:2.

For too long, I had no understanding of the truth hidden in the last phrase of Psalm 138:2. I had always assumed that it meant God's word was important to him and should be to me also, but I had no idea if it had some specific significance other than giving us a vague sense of the value God placed on his word. Because I didn't immediately get what the phrase was saying, I ignored it and focused instead on the "loving kindness and truth" part.

The Bible was telling me that God has magnified his word above all his name, but I didn't even ask, "So what?" Meanwhile, a nugget of truth lay there undiscovered, like gold on an unexplored riverbed.

On that sleepless night in February when I heard what Bill Johnson said, I knew he had caught sight of that glimmer of gold and I remembered the day I had first seen it, several years earlier. And I lay there, reliving "The Day of the Glimmer."

THE DAY OF THE GLIMMER

I think we all love the psalms. Perhaps we see our own journey reflected in the lives of the psalmists. There is something very familiar about their cries for help mingled with their assertions of—and thanks for—God's faithfulness. I confess that as I witness their sometimes failing but always renewed hope in God's goodness, I identify; and I experience that renewal with them. The ancient songs of these very human worshipers turn my own eyes away from my trouble or weakness and back to the one from whom "my help cometh".

Years before the wakeful night I just wrote about, I developed the habit of reading aloud from the psalms during my devotions. One morning, I had just declared from verse two of Psalm 138, "I thank you that you have magnified your word above all your name," when I stopped, embarrassed. Britches ripped again!

I thank you for what?

Suddenly—probably a result of my fertile imagination—this disconcerting picture flashed into my mind: God listening, and knowing I had no idea what I was saying.

I was embarrassed. Did I think I could impress God by spouting lovely words when he knew I didn't have a clue what they meant?

I have to admit this next step was taken more to cover my embarrassment than for any other reason. I prayed sheepishly, "God, I don't know what that means. Could you show me?"

By that time in my life, I had discovered that if I asked God for understanding of scripture, I would eventually get my answer—for the most part anyway—from my pastor's sermons, from a teacher on television, from a book, or even from a friend over a steaming cup at Starbuck's. Not always though, I admit, and this was one of those times when illumination didn't come even after quite some time.

But this time I wasn't willing to give up.

After that, I would pray that same prayer whenever I read Psalm 138:2, no doubt because I was still embarrassed about that "meaningless praise" incident.

As months passed, my motivation for the prayer changed. I became convinced of two things: first, the information held in that little verse was an important key to my understanding "the loving kindness and truth" of God; and second, there was something about that loving kindness I needed to know.

Embarrassment was soon replaced by dogged determination. There was gold in them thar' hills, and I planned to find it.

There's an interesting verse found in the New Testament: "Ask (and keep on asking) and it shall be given you; seek (and keep on seeking) and ye shall find," (Mark 7:7). Mark's record of Jesus' words showed me that God doesn't mind a nag.

So I nagged.

Finally, one day, after I had prayed yet again, "Lord, I still don't understand how you can magnify your word above your name, but your Holy Spirit is my teacher, so I thank you that he will show me what it means," I had this thought: *You know what my word is; study the name.*

Study the name?

I felt as if I were being sidetracked from my objective. After all, I was curious about the magnified word, not the name. But then, what did I have to lose? At least I was on the move.

Later, I was reading from Proverbs when this verse told me what my first step would have to be: "My son, if thou wilt *receive my words,* and hide my commandments with thee; So that thou incline thine ear unto wisdom, and *apply thine heart to understanding*; yea, if thou cryest after knowledge, and liftest up thy voice for understanding; if thou seekest for her as for silver, and *searchest for her as for hid treasures*; then shalt thou understand the fear of the Lord and find the knowledge of God," (Proverbs 2:1-5).

As I read those words, I flashed back to the dusty grounds of Camp Emmanuel, the church camp that gave me the best two weeks of summer vacation for most of my formative years.

CAMP EMMANUEL

Nestled on a hill and valley on Canada's east coast, on the island of Newfoundland, the cluster of cabins, dorms, diner, tabernacle, and unforgettable outhouses overlooked the shining waters of Conception Bay, where the air was the sweetest breathed on God's earth.

Now, in my mind, a scene played out that had taken place there, back in the sixties. I held the autograph book I had bought at the Book Nook's Last Day Sale to catch those "last words" from my friends before we headed home. On its pastel pages—between the "Friends 4 ever" over one friend's name and address, and the "2 sweet 2 be 4 gotten" penned by another—my Daily Vacation Bible School teacher had scrawled a Bible verse. He had written simply, "Study to show thyself approved unto God, a workman that needeth not to be ashamed, rightly dividing the word of truth," (2 Timothy 2:15). Underneath he had signed his name, Lindahl Faulkner. I could still remember the slight uneasiness I'd felt as I read his words.

Lindahl—whose impact on me can be measured by the fact that he's the only DVBS teacher whose face I can clearly recall—had spent two weeks teaching from the book of Jude and had taken every opportunity to remind us that we had been handed a wonderful treasure, the "faith once delivered to the saints." With fire in his eyes he challenged us to handle this treasure with care.

Looking back now, I realize that my uneasiness about what he had written came from the fact that I subscribed to the "I don't cuss and I don't chew and I don't kiss the boys that do" brand of Christianity, otherwise known, when one becomes proficient, as "Miss Goody Two Shoes Syndrome". In other words, I would try to live as good a life as I knew how and hope my effort would bring me whatever approval I needed.

My denomination's tenets of faith included salvation by grace but, somehow, I didn't quite *get* it. I didn't get that I had been approved of God—that my "right standing" in his eyes had been established—the moment I had accepted Jesus' sacrifice for my sin and called him Lord.

My confusion may have arisen because the youth leaders during my teen years—Lindahl being a notable exception—in an honorable effort to encourage young believers to make right decisions, focused a great deal on what actions would be pleasing to God. Perhaps as a result of that, I developed my own concept of "salvation by works." Consequently, to my mind, the verse Lindahl had just written in my autograph book read like this: "Study so that God will approve you."

Whatever the reason, I felt like this admonition from the book of Timothy gave me another requirement I had to meet for my salvation, and I knew I would fall short. I hated the shame of falling short; hence, the uneasiness.

Now, many years later—in Proverbs this time—here it was again: a challenge to engage.

This time, however, I was better equipped to handle the challenge. I knew my ultimate goal wasn't to gain approval but, rather, to gain understanding—the kind God gives. A very precious commodity! Life had already shown me how precious and how very necessary that kind of understanding is.

Now, too, I understood the fire I had seen decades before in my teacher's eyes, and this new challenge brought no uneasiness.

Instead, there was anticipation of something good. There was hidden treasure to be uncovered; silver and gold to be found.

Proverbs called me to an adventure, a search for the treasure in Psalm 138:2. I would find it as I studied "the name".

Now, having picked up this book, you are called to the same adventure—the journey I began several years before the night Bill Johnson asked that question.

Thomas Cahill, in his book *How the Irish Saved Civilization*, describes St. Augustine's conversion to Christianity. Cahill tells how Augustine began to read Paul's writings and came to the conclusion that "if we mud-spattered human beings are ever to ascend to Truth, we can do it only because God, a force greater than our war-torn selves, has predestined us and calls us upward."

God has made his truth available to all of us mud-spattered souls, and calls us all to seek it—to seek him.

And any call from God is an upward call!

Thinking about Chapter One

SELF DISCOVERY QUESTIONS:

1. What does Psalm 138:2 mean to you?
2. Do you feel uneasy about being called to this adventure? If so, why?
3. Are you willing to take this journey?

TRUTH CHASER'S PRAYER:

Father God,

Please wake up the truth chaser in me. Help me to be willing, always, to follow you on any journey. Thank you for the guidance which comes so faithfully from your Holy Spirit. And thank you, ahead of time, for being patient with me.

CHAPTER TWO

They That Know Thy Name

"It is not the critic who counts; not the man who points out where the strong man stumbles or where the doer of deeds could have done them better. The credit belongs to the man who is actually in the arena, whose face is marred by dust and sweat and blood: who strives valiantly: who errs, and comes short again and again; because there is not effort without error and shortcoming; but who does actually strive to do the deeds; who knows the great enthusiasms, the great devotions; who spends himself in a worthy cause, who at the best knows in the end the triumphs of high achievement and who at the worst, if he fails, at least fails while daring greatly, so that his place shall never be with those cold and timid souls who know neither victory or defeat."

THEODORE ROOSEVELT
Speech: The Man In The Arena
Sorbonne, April 23, 1910.

2.

"They that know thy name will put their trust in thee,
for thou Lord hast not forsaken them
that seek thee." ~ Psalm 9:10

My quest for knowledge of the name brought me, before long, to a signpost, Psalm 9:10. Apparently, according to this verse of scripture, knowing God's name is a confidence-in-God builder. It follows, therefore, that people who know God's name carry an identifying trademark: trust in God.

It occurred to me that if I could study people who displayed confidence in God I would find out what they knew about him—or about his name—that influenced their level of trust.

If I could walk with them through their most challenging experiences, watching them carefully and listening to what they had to say, I might find out exactly what did motivate and empower them.

Abraham quickly came to mind, as did King David and the three Hebrew children. Although the acts for which we remember them were definitely out of the ordinary and probably brought them a few critics at the time, it was pretty clear they all trusted God.

According to my signpost, that meant they must have known God's name. I decided, therefore, that they would be able mentors and suitable models for me in my search for knowledge of "the name." Their stories are, indeed, instructive and inspiring.

ABRAHAM'S STORY

One of Abraham's stories is told in Genesis 22. God had given Abraham a son and had told him, "In Isaac shall thy seed be called." In other words, the promise God had given Abraham—that he would be a father of many nations—would be fulfilled through Isaac. A problem arose later when God instructed Abraham to sacrifice Isaac as a burnt offering. Unthinkably, Isaac, the son of promise, was to be killed on an altar in the land of Moriah!

Tradition suggests that this command to sacrifice Isaac was a test of Abraham's love, obedience, or commitment to the Lord God. Of course, he passed.

All right, he's our mentor so let's watch closely. Just how did Abraham respond to God's command? How did he pass what must have been a profoundly painful test? Where did he find the strength to obey?

The book of Hebrews tells us what was going on in Abraham's mind and heart:

> Hebrews 11:17-19 "By faith Abraham, when he was tried, offered up Isaac: and he that received the promises offered up his only begotten son, Of whom it was said, That in Isaac shall thy seed be called: accounting that God was able to raise him up, even from the dead; from hence he received him in a figure."

It would seem Abraham *expected* God to bring Isaac back from the dead. The reference to the promise indicates as much.

But even if Hebrews' reference to the promise doesn't necessarily mean Abraham was still expecting its fulfillment, Abraham's comments to his servants definitely suggest as much. Before he left them to climb the mountain, he said, "I and the lad will go yonder and worship, and come to you again." Unless he was lying to his servants—and why would he bother?—Abraham expected Isaac to return with him.

One morning during devotions at a Christian high school, I talked about Abraham's almost incredible expectation. I was shocked by a vehement response from one of the students. Appalled that I would suggest Abraham's obedience could have been influenced by anything other than self-sacrifice and love for God, he refused to believe that Abraham expected God to raise Isaac up.

Taken aback by his response, I wondered why, in the face of considerable Biblical evidence to the contrary, he would be so adamant in his denial that Abraham believed God would raise Isaac from the dead.

I concluded that maybe we find it easier to emulate Abraham's obedience—his willingness to sacrifice his best for God—than his belief that God would keep his promises.

The indicators suggest that Abraham continued to hold fast to the promise that said "in Isaac shall thy seed be called" even in the face of its apparent denial. He "that received the promises" believed God's promise about Isaac, and offered up his only begotten son "accounting that God was able to raise him up". Amazing!

We, on the other hand, often back down when confronted with circumstances that conflict with the promises given to us.

Why do we do that? Why are we so quick to let go of specific promises God has made? Or why do we find it difficult to hold fast to them confidently?

After all, not only do we have a written record of the many promises of God, we've also read how God redeemed us from what the Bible calls "the authority of darkness" by sacrificing Jesus on the cross. And this because he loved us!

Most of us would never doubt his love. Yet, sometimes we struggle to believe that these promises made by our greatest lover will be fulfilled.

So what did Abraham know that we don't know?

DAVID'S STORY

In 1 Samuel 17, we find what is possibly the most famous of David's stories. It happened when David was still a young man, long before anyone sang songs of his bravery and skill in battle. His father had sent him to take food to his brothers who were at the battle site where the Philistines and their trump card, the formidable warrior-giant, Goliath, held King Saul and the men of Israel at a standstill.

As a young shepherd, David had spent a lot of time on the hillsides caring for his father's sheep. No doubt, during many long days and nights when the quiet was interrupted only by the bleating of the sheep and the occasional pesky predator, David meditated on the God of his fathers.

We know he spent time thinking about God on those hills, not just because of the worship songs he wrote then, but also because of what immediately came to his mind when he saw what was happening in the valley of Elah.

There was supposed to be a battle going on, but there wasn't.

Hear the outrage in his voice:

Vs. 26 "Who is this uncircumcised Philistine, that he should defy the armies of the living God?"

David saw the men of Israel cowering in the presence of trouble and knew there was something wrong with this scene. This man, Goliath of Gath, was uncircumcised. That meant that he had no covenant with God—that God had made him no promises. Yet, the children of Israel, possessors of the promises, were the fearful ones.

It was unthinkable.

David began to tell everyone around him, "God will deliver us from this scourge!"

This annoyed his older brother who scolded him for his insolence and presumption. David replied, "What have I done? Is there not a cause?" In other words, "Don't I have reason to say these things, considering our covenant?"

The impassioned young shepherd preached his message to any and all who would listen. Eventually, the soldiers took him to King Saul himself. With vivid accounts of his past victories by God's hand—the stories about the lions and bears that tried and failed to steal his sheep—David attempted to persuade Saul to let him face the bone-chilling Goliath.

It worked!

I've often wondered what Saul saw in David's eyes or heard in his voice that made him decide to send him out—a boy against a giant, a singing shepherd against a proven warrior. Whatever it was, I'll bet Goliath saw it in David's fearless run toward him on the field of battle. Or perhaps he heard it in David's shout: "You came to me with a sword, and with a spear, and with a shield: but I come to you in the name of the Lord of hosts, the God of the armies of Israel, whom thou hast defied" (Verse 45).

Have you ever wondered where courage like that comes from? Could it simply be that, like Abraham, David had a promise he expected to be fulfilled?

One of God's promises to His people was deliverance from their enemies. Deuteronomy 28:7 says, "The Lord shall cause thine enemies that rise up against thee to be smitten before thy face: they shall come out against thee one way, and flee before thee seven ways."

Certainly, David must have known that promise because here's what he shouted to the threatening Goliath in verse 46: "This day will the Lord deliver thee into mine hand; and I will smite thee."

In this one amazing statement I hear David's confidence that God would uphold the words recorded in Deuteronomy 28: "thine enemies…smitten before thy face."

That same verse told him his enemies would flee before him seven ways.

And they did flee. Verse 51 in 1 Samuel 17 tells us, "and when the Philistines saw their champion was dead, they fled."

THE THREE HEBREW CHILDREN'S STORY

The story of Shadrach, Meshach, and Abednego is told in Chapter Three of the book of Daniel.

Daniel 3:14-18 "Nebuchadnezzar spoke and said unto them, Is it true, O Shadrach, Meshach, and Abednego, do not ye serve my gods, nor worship the golden image which I have set up? Now if ye be ready that at what time ye hear the sound of the cornet, flute, harp, sackbut, psaltery, and dulcimer, and all kinds of music, ye fall down and worship the image I have made, well: but if ye worship not, ye shall be cast the same hour into the midst of a fiery furnace; and who is that God that shall deliver you out of my hands? Shadrach, Meshach, and Abednego, answered and said to the king, O Nebuchadnezzar, we are not careful to answer thee in this matter. *If it be so,* our God whom we serve is able to deliver us from the burning fiery furnace, and he will deliver us out of thine hand, O king. *But if not,* be it known unto thee, O king, that we will not serve thy gods, nor worship the golden image which thou hast set up." [Italics added]

How we love the rest of the story! They were thrown into the flames, but suddenly, miraculously, they were joined by a big fellow who looked so powerful he appeared to be "like the son of God." Then, wonder of wonders, the four of them walked freely in the fire.

When the king saw this, he had an immediate conversion experience. Not surprising, since whenever someone who looks like the son of God shows up in a conflict, you definitely want to be found on his side!

Whatever Nebuchadnezzar's motivation might have been—change of heart or survival instinct—he altered his furnace policy. Listen to him as he tells our sweet-smelling, no-smoke-on-them young heroes to "come hither" out of the fire.

Vs. 28 "Then Nebuchadnezzar spake and said, Blessed be the God of Shadrach, Meshach, and Abednego, who hath sent his angel, and delivered his servants that trusted in him...and yielded their bodies that they might not serve nor worship any god except their own God."

In this case, as with Abraham, God delivered his children even when it looked as if all hope was lost.

Some have told this familiar story to encourage us to be dedicated and obedient to God even in the face of adversity. To be sure, such dedication and obedience are admirable, and possibly even necessary.

However, sometimes we have been led to believe, inadvertently but definitely incorrectly, that those three brave boys went into the flames thinking God might not help them.

This misconception no doubt comes from the words recorded in verses 17 and 18 when the boys said to the king, "Our God will deliver us...but if not, we will not serve your gods."

But that, in fact, is not what this passage is saying. When we listen to the boys carefully, we realize they were convinced God would deliver them. Others may have thought all hope was lost, but not these young Hebrews. See here what they really said:

> Vs. 17 *"If it be so,* our god whom we serve is able to deliver us from the fiery furnace, and he will deliver us out of thine hand O king."

If what be so? If the king's threat be so! The boys were saying they doubted the king's ability to carry out his threat. Here's the king's threat:

> Vs. 15 "If ye worship not, ye shall be cast that same hour into the midst of a burning fiery furnace."

In verse 17, they are telling the king that if he throws them in the furnace, "our God *can* and *will* deliver us out of your hand." According to this, they didn't doubt either God's ability *or* His willingness to deliver them.

Let's look at verses 17 and 18 together:

> *"If it be so* (that is, if you throw us in the furnace) our God *can* and *will* deliver us from your hand. *But if not* (that is, if you do not throw us in the furnace), we still will not bow down and worship the image."

In other words: "No negotiation! No deal!"

Why would they say "Our God will deliver us" as well as "Our God can deliver us"? Of course, they had heard the stories of the great deliverances of the past and had seen the hand of God deliver their people more than once. History told them God *could* deliver, but what made them say he *will*?

Could it have been because of something else they knew?

We can assume they knew the scriptures. We saw evidence of that in their diligent and meticulous efforts to obey the law. Remember, they had earlier refused to eat the king's food because their covenant told them it was unlawful.

Surely, then, they would have also known that God had said, "When thou passest through the waters I will be with thee: when thou walkest through the fire, thou shalt not be burned; neither shall the flame kindle upon thee" (Isaiah 43:2).

They probably also recalled verses from Psalms that told of God's willingness to deliver all who fear him. Psalm 34:7, for example, says, "The angel of the Lord encampeth round about them that fear him and delivereth them." The only proviso of this promise was fear of God and it is obvious from their actions that they feared God. That's how they got into this trouble in the first place: obedience to God's directive to worship no other gods—an obedience no doubt born out of a proper fear and respect for God.

They knew the commandments and they knew the promises. Is there something else Shadrach, Meshach, and Abednego could have known that made them say God *will*, and not just God *can*?

Is it possible they are saying in verse 17 that they, like Abraham and David before them, expected God to do exactly what he said?

What About Us?

Many of us, like them, know what's been promised to us. We have "exceeding great and precious promises, whereby we are partakers of the divine nature" (2 Peter 1:4). Like David and the three Hebrews, we too have heard the stories that have preceded ours over the many generations since the days of Abraham—stories of great exploits done by people who knew their God. Yet, many of us still cower when a mountain hinders or a giant, someone or some circumstance bigger than us, threatens.

Of course we cower, you say; we're human.

Yes, we are. So were they. They were not mythical characters; they were people just like us.

In Daniel 11:32, we are told "they that know their God" will be strong and do "exploits". We can no doubt agree that the few men we have studied here, as well as many men and women elsewhere in the Bible, were strong and did exploits. Have you ever wondered why these people who weren't indwelt by the Holy Spirit appear stronger than we seem to be—we, who have been given the Comforter?

We have a covenant too. A better covenant, we're told, based on better promises. Yet, not many of us can claim the spiritual strength evidenced in these stories.

I wonder if it's partly because in the telling of these stories to our children in Sunday school, or even in our pulpits to our adult congregations, we tend to make heroes of the people—and, really, they did have qualities we recognize as heroic. We admire them for their courage, faith, obedience, and self-sacrifice. All qualities we need and wish we had.

No doubt, the stories, like the songs we sang in Sunday School—Remember "Dare to be a Daniel"?—are told so that we will imitate the heroes, as well we should! Both songs and stories are meant to motivate us to be courageous, trust God, and be obedient.

Sometimes we're just intimidated.

Perhaps it is when we feel most inadequate that the "I don't cuss and I don't chew" philosophy appears so attractive. It's much less demanding, we think, than giant slaying.

Of course, it *is* less demanding. It's also less glorious. To my knowledge, there are no songs which celebrate a quite admirable abstinence from cussing and chewing!

Could our focus be off?

In looking at these heroes of the faith, is it possible that we come away not really seeing the true hero of those stories—our loving, faithful, strong and mighty God?

Is there something else we need to know about God before we can be bold and do exploits like these great men of old?

Listen to them again.

Abraham: *"I and the lad will return."*

David: *"This day the Lord will deliver thee into my hand."*

Three Hebrews: *"Our God can and will deliver us."*

Such certainty!

I've heard it said that these men of Old Testament times had supernatural boldness because the Holy Spirit came upon them to enable them to do something out of the ordinary for God. There have been times I've wanted to believe it. After all, it would mean my ineffectiveness could be excused by a lack of special anointing, and, I confess, my natural tendency is to opt for any explanations of scripture that leave me in my comfort zone.

But if it were true, wouldn't the book that is "profitable for doctrine" say so? Wouldn't it say of them, as it does of others, that "the spirit of the Lord came upon them and they prophesied" declaring their victory in advance? One might think it should since the Author is interested in our correct doctrine.

But it doesn't, and we shouldn't presume it happened that way.

Comfort must always give way to truth.

If it wasn't some special anointing that empowered them, what was it that made them do the great exploits we have read about? Did Abraham, David, Shadrach, Meshach, and Abednego simply know—better than we do—what a hero God is?

Thinking about Chapter Two

SELF DISCOVERY QUESTIONS:

1. Do you feel you know God's name?
2. Do you have the same confidence in God that the Bible heroes had?
3. Do you think it would it be prideful to say you had such confidence in God?
4. Are there certain words or promises from God which you have clung to in times of trouble?

TRUTH CHASER'S PRAYER:

Dear Father,

I confess I love my comfort zone. I admit I can't imagine doing anything remotely like the courageous acts I read about in your word. I can't even imagine you'd want me to do them. But I know there must be something you want me to do. Something I can only do with your help. If so, I may need to know you as David and Abraham did, and as those three young Hebrew boys did. So please help me. Help me to know your name.

CHAPTER THREE

What's In A Name?

"What's in a name?
That which we call
by any other name
would smell as sweet."

WILLIAM SHAKESPEARE
Romeo and Juliet

3.

"*Then they that feared the Lord spake often one to another: and the Lord hearkened, and heard it, and a book of remembrance was written before him for them that feared the Lord, and that thought upon his name, and they shall be mine, saith the Lord of hosts, in that day when I make up my jewels.*"
- *Malachi 3:16-17*

Imagine yourself with the same kind of courage and confidence in God we've just read about. It must be possible. Those men weren't some super-spiritual breed. They must have been ordinary people, just like us, because they certainly had the same human frailties we have.

Think about David's life. As well as his spiritual, physical and ethical victories, don't the words "adultery" and "murder" come to mind? Human frailties were David's constant companions.

Abraham had them, too. As well as the times Abraham made heroic and faithful choices, there were a couple of moments that were remarkable only for their apparent cowardice as he effectively hid behind his wife, presenting her as his sister so no one would kill him in order to have her.

Obviously, theirs was not a special trust in God found only in the hearts of heroes. In fact, it seems that whatever heroism they displayed actually sprang from their trust in God, not the other way around.

We saw earlier where that trust came from. The signpost, Psalm 9:10, indicates that their trust was born of their knowledge of God, and—if the psalmist is to be believed—anyone who knows God's name will trust him like that.

After all, we have the same God. A businessman from New York has the same God as an ancient, nomadic new believer from Ur of the Chaldees. A homemaker in Dallas has the same God as a teenage shepherd on the hills near Bethlehem. An office worker in Toronto can know the same God as three Israeli slaves facing annihilation in the ancient land that is now Iraq. Surely, if we really knew his name, we could have the same trust in him.

Are you ready for that chase I mentioned?

It begins here.

TRAIL ONE: THE NAMES OF GOD

The names of God reveal who he is and what he intends his relationship with us to be: our Shepherd, Righteousness, Healer, Victory, Peace, Ever-present One, and so on. These were what first came to mind when I began my study of the name. However, after following that trail for some time, I was no further ahead in understanding Psalm 138:2. Why would God magnify his word above the names which represent his promised covenant relationship with his children? It just didn't make sense.

I knew this trail couldn't be the right one because when the Holy Spirit, the great teacher of the church, illuminates God's word we need no mental gymnastics or suspension of disbelief to make sense of it.

Daunted at first, I eventually decided there had to be another route. There had to be another use of the word "name" that would work in that verse and make its meaning clear. The chase continued on another trail.

TRAIL TWO: ANY MAN'S NAME

It occurred to me that God gave us the ability to use words and communicates with us through words. The specific words he uses to communicate himself and his ways are, therefore, important and worth scrutiny. I also realized that we sometimes spiritualize

Biblical language, inadvertently removing it from any connection to our everyday usage. In doing so, we might create a hindrance to our understanding.

For these two reasons, with my goal of studying the name, I finally asked Shakespeare's famous question, "What's in a name?"

I concluded that if I could clarify in my own mind the implications of anyone's name, as well as different ways the word "name" is used, perhaps I would understand more of what is meant by the name of the Lord. I decided to find out how the word "name" is used elsewhere in the Bible as well as in our own daily usage. That, I thought, might shed some light on its use in Psalm 138:2.

So, the search began. It was a well-trodden path and easy to follow.

IDENTIFICATION
"Her name is Gillian Elizabeth."

The scene: Grace Maternity Hospital in Halifax, Nova Scotia. Our beautiful baby daughter had, but an hour or two earlier, made her earth debut. My husband and I were thrilled and wanted to call our family and friends throughout Canada to tell of her safe arrival.

There was, however, a problem: For some reason, I was convinced we were having a boy—a boy whom I had called Richard for many months already. Instead, here was a sweet baby girl.

I was thrilled by this development, but I wasn't prepared for it. Richard was the only name we had thought of. And now Glenn refused to make a call until she had a name, protesting, "It just doesn't seem right to introduce her without a name."

Such a fuss about a name! At that moment I didn't really care! But inspiration came: "Her name is Gillian Elizabeth." No longer vaguely identified as "Baby Rowe", she had her own distinctive name. Her proud daddy made the calls.

Obviously, the first thing a name does is give the simplest of answers to the question, "Who are you?" Identification is the most basic purpose of a name. Even God identified himself by giving his name.

As the story in Exodus goes, God had just instructed Moses to go to his people in Egypt and lead them out of that country and out of slavery. Moses knew he would be called upon to identify the source of his authority and power and, in so doing, legitimize his claim that he had been sent to bring the children of Israel out of Egypt.

Moses says to God, "They'll ask who sent me. They'll say, 'what is his name?'"

The answer came.

"And God said unto Moses, I AM THAT I AM: and he said, Thus shall thou say unto the children of Israel, 'I AM hath sent me unto you,'" (Exodus 3:14).

There, Moses. That's who is backing you up. The one whose name is I AM.

CHARACTER
"YOU CAN'T TELL A BOOK BY ITS COVER."

Outward appearances can be deceiving, and even though we often judge someone by looks, clothing, job or family name, we can recognize the folly inherent in that practice.

The truth is, if all we know is someone's external persona, we know very little. To really know someone, we need to know his character. Since we can't see into someone's heart and mind, we determine a person's character through words and actions. Proverbs 20:11 says, "Even a child is known by his doings, whether his work be pure, and whether it be right."

It's simple. We know character by actions. When someone's actions result in good for other people, we say he is kind; when his words and actions agree, we say he has integrity; when he speaks the truth as he knows it, we say he is honest. On the other hand, if someone we have known to be honest appears to have lied, we say the action is *out of character* for that individual.

And so it goes. It's the same for everyone. In fact, Psalm 9:16 says, "The Lord is known by the judgment which he executeth."

Even God is known by his actions.

This knowledge of someone's actions and the resulting perception of character is part of what creates a reputation, a hugely significant aspect of one's name.

REPUTATION
"YOUR REPUTATION HAS EXCEEDED YOU."

A few years ago, my family and I were members of a church whose pastor often traveled to minister in other churches. On one occasion, he was invited to preach in one of the largest churches of that denomination in America. The service was going to be televised across much of the nation and he told our church family to be sure to watch.

When he came to the pulpit on the big day, he told that congregation how honored he was to have been invited to minister to them. Obviously intending to say, "Your reputation has preceded you," he said instead, "Your reputation has exceeded you."

The following Sunday in our own service, with solemn countenance but tongue in cheek, he invited us all to repent for laughing at him. He suggested his wife lead the way.

This story reminds me of the message to the angel at the church in Sardis: "thou hast a name that thou livest, and art dead," (Revelation 3:1). Although their name literally meant "living" in this case their reputation really had exceeded them!

We often refer to the reputation of a person, product, or company by the word "name." We say, "That ministry/person/company/product has a good name—or not as the case might be. We don't mean there is something especially nice or nasty about the word by which they are identified. We are talking about their reputation. Proverbs 22:1 refers to this aspect of one's name: "A good name is rather to be chosen than great riches."

In the business world, a good name might well bring great riches, so marketers are all about reputation. They try to create the impression their product is consistently good and worthy of the consumer's trust. That is part of what is known as "branding."

These same marketers know the importance of quality control so that the product is, in fact, consistently good and all that it claims to be, because if there is no substance to claims made in marketing hype, consumers won't believe in the product and won't trust it. And they'll spread the word. Marketers know that one person's negative experience, if reported, is all that's needed for the rest of the public to distrust a product or company. When a company's name is not good, it may take some time and forgetfulness for us to buy the product again—or indeed any product from that manufacturer.

Reputation is powerful—so much so that the concept of branding is not limited to goods and services. Personal branding has come to the forefront in today's competitive, internet-connected environment where careers in the public arena stand or fall on the opinions of others. Some people have engaged in deliberately misleading personal branding, giving spin doctors a challenging job. Eventually the truth does "out" and these people wear the brand they have earned.

There are others, of course, whose brand develops naturally over time. One great example among these natural brands is Dr. Billy Graham. Dr. Graham's brand of sincerity, wisdom, and integrity has given him the ear of many leaders in the worlds of religion and politics, and has also given him a place of great influence among Christians worldwide.

So what does all this have to do with God's name?

Just this: God knew—long before our twenty-first century marketers and publicists—that being known and being positively perceived is important. The Bible shows us the connection. Psalm 76:1 says, "in Judah God is known: his name is great in Israel."

In Psalm 78, we see that God gave specific instructions to the children of Israel to ensure that he would continue to be known. They were to pass God's stories on to their children, telling them about his mighty acts toward his people.

Psalm 78: 4-7 "We will not hide them from our children, shewing to the generation to come the praises of the Lord, and his strength, and his wonderful works that he hath done. For he established a testimony in Jacob, and appointed a law in Israel, which he commanded our fathers, that they should make them known to their children: That the generation to come might know them, even the children which should be born; who should arise and declare them to their children: That they might set their hope in God, and not forget the works of God and keep his commandments."

Obviously, God cares about his reputation. That's why it has always been important to God that he be represented accurately in the earth. When God's works are reported accurately, his reputation—his name—is very great.

FOR HIS NAME'S SAKE

Not only does God care about his reputation, he guards it carefully. There are many incidents recorded in the Bible where God takes a particular action or refrains from action "for his name sake." Several of these occurred in the wilderness when the children of Israel turned away from God's directions in ways that could have legally resulted in their immediate demise.

The records of these events can be found in Exodus, Psalms, and Ezekiel. One was when Moses was on Mount Sinai receiving the Ten Commandments.

Because Moses was gone so long, the Israelites became very anxious. Fearful and stressed, they reverted to what they had seen in Egypt, building and worshiping a golden calf, hoping that this new "god" would help them.

God was angry. He told Moses he was ready to wipe out the rebellious lot and start over. Exodus 32:10 tells us how close the Israelites were to destruction as God said, "Let me alone...that I may consume them: and I will make of thee a great nation."

Exodus 32:12, 13 tells us Moses "besought the Lord his God and said, Wherefore should the Egyptians speak and say, For mischief did he bring them out, to slay them in the mountains, and to consume them from the face of the earth? ... Remember Abraham, Isaac, and Israel, thy servants, to whom thou swearest by thine own self and saidst to them, I will multiply your seed as the stars of heaven, and all this land that I have spoken of will I give unto your seed and they shall inherit it forever."

Moses' response to God has been the subject of a fair bit of discussion: Who was Moses to contradict God?

Maybe he wasn't contradicting God—or even being unfathomably cheeky! Remember, Moses knew God's ways, not just his acts. When he reminded God of his promise to Abraham, Isaac, and Jacob, he merely exhibited the same confidence in God that we saw earlier in our other heroes—confidence in God's commitment to the covenant. Then, knowing that this people had actually earned their destruction and that God could legally, within covenant terms, start over with a new nation, Moses reminded him of how his proposed course of action would look to the Egyptians.

Apparently the latter worked. In Ezekiel we get an even clearer picture of why God didn't give the rebellious house of Israel what their actions called for:

> Ezekiel 20:13-14 "But the house of Israel rebelled against me in the wilderness: they walked not in my statutes, and they despised my judgments, which if a man do he shall even live in them; and my Sabbaths they greatly polluted: then I said, I would pour out my fury upon them in the wilderness, to consume them, But I wrought (acted) for my name sake, that It (my name) should not be polluted before the heathen, in whose sight I brought them out."

They deserved destruction but God saved them for his name sake. Psalm 106: 7, 8 confirms God's desire to preserve his reputation throughout the Israelites' wilderness journey: "Our fathers understood not thy wonders in Egypt; they remembered not the multitude of thy mercies; but provoked him at the Red Sea. Nevertheless, he saved them for his name sake, that he might make his mighty power known."

For his name sake, God preserved their lives!

AUTHORITY
"Stop in the name of the law"

If you recognize that command, you were probably raised in the days of cheesy Saturday morning westerns, as was I. The familiar scene on the black and white television usually involved a runaway bad guy dressed in black and pursued by a sheriff—the latter wearing a white hat and wielding a Colt six-shooter. The small badge on the sheriff's vest was all that showed he wasn't acting on his own authority, so he shouted his command, "…in the name of the law!"

Somehow, the words didn't sound quite so corny when John Wayne ruled the West.

Sheriff John Wayne wasn't operating in his own authority in arresting the bad guy. He had "the law" behind him—and, with that law, the power that would back it up.

But, truth be told, every name carries a degree of authority with it and there are many possible bases for our authority.

One obvious one is that we have authority over things we own. We can make decisions about our homes that someone else cannot make because our name on a title deed gives us authority over property, and our name on a bank account says we are the only one who can legally access the funds in it.

In fact, every time we sign our name on a document we are using and expressing our authority.

Another place we have authority is within the realm of our responsibility. For example, our authority over our children is inextricably connected to our responsibility for their training and welfare. This story about my daughter illustrates the point.

Once, when Gillian was about five or six, she and her little friend were playing in our backyard. The lawn was covered with playhouse paraphernalia, including Gillian's baby bathtub. From inside the house, I heard the girls giggling and recognized something in their tone that said, "Check this out!" I ran to the window and looked out into the adjacent yard. Horrified, I saw the girls stripping a gorgeous rhododendron bush—my neighbors' pride and joy—of every last blossom, gleefully piling them into that tub.

I ran outside to rescue whatever was left on that shrub from the hands of my own little pride and joy. I sent Gillian's friend home and Gillian to her room to meditate on the gravity of her transgression. Later, the other little girl's mother called to say, "You aren't going to tell [my neighbor] who did this, are you?"

I assured her I would leave her daughter's name out of it, but told her that when our neighbors returned from work Gillian would be going next door to admit what she had done and apologize.

I was responsible for Gillian, and my authority over her was, in my opinion, divinely connected to my responsibility for her training. In this instance I had to take advantage of the opportunity to teach her to accept the consequences of her actions. Even though I thought Gillian's friend should share the consequence, I had no authority to ensure she did.

All authority—whatever might be its reason or origin—can be transferred or delegated. As parents, for example, we routinely give teachers and babysitters a limited measure of authority over our children. As well, someone who holds our power of attorney can access our bank account. And we should remember this at election time: when we vote, we delegate authority and, with it, the power and responsibility to exercise that authority.

Authority is not just a legal concept. It is a spiritual concept, in ways that many of us find almost incomprehensible. But the Bible makes it clear.

GOD'S DELEGATED AUTHORITY

Even God delegates authority—and backs it up with his power.

We know he has authority and why. Psalm 24:1 tells us, "The earth is the Lord's, and the fullness thereof; the world and they that dwell therein." Verse 2 tells us why he owns the earth, "For he hath founded it...and established it." God owns what he's created, he has authority over it, and he has the right to delegate that authority wherever he wishes.

Psalms speaks to one aspect of authority God gave man: "Thou madest him to have dominion over the works of thy hands, and hast put all things under his feet" (Psalm 8:6) and "The heaven, even the heavens, are the Lord's: but the earth hath he given to the children of men" (Psalm 115:16).

God put things of the earth in man's hands. In the New Testament we see an example of delegation of his authority in an even greater way. In the next references "the name above all names" refers to Jesus. These verses show that the phrase refers to his authority:

Philippians 2:9-11 (referring to Jesus) "Wherefore, God has highly exalted him, and given him a name which is above every name: that at the name of Jesus every knee should bow, of things in heaven, and things in earth, and things under the earth; And that every tongue should confess that Jesus Christ is Lord, to the glory of God the Father."

Ephesians 1:15-22 "Wherefore I also, after I heard of your faith in the Lord Jesus Christ, and love to all the saints cease not to make mention of you in my prayers; that the God of our Lord Jesus Christ, the Father of glory, may give unto you the spirit of wisdom and revelation in the knowledge of him: the eyes of your understanding being enlightened; that ye may know what is the hope of his calling, and what the riches of the glory of his inheritance in the saints, and what is the exceeding greatness of his power to us-ward who believe, according to the working of his mighty power, which he wrought in Christ when he raised him from the dead, and set him at his own right hand in the heavenly places, far above all principality and power, and might, and dominion, and every name that is named, not only in this world but in the world to come: and put all things under his feet, and gave him to be the head over all things to the church."

In Mark 16:17, we see Jesus commissioning his disciples and giving them the authority to use his name. He says, "In my name shall they cast out devils." He was telling his disciples to go, not in their own right or power to rule in the situations they encountered, but in his right and power to rule. He was delegating authority.

In Acts 3, we see Peter acting on Jesus' word. He says to the lame man at the gate of the temple, in response to being asked for a gift, "What I have I give thee: In the name of Jesus Christ of Nazareth, rise up and walk." Notice that Peter refers to something that he, himself, has. He says, "What I have, I give thee."

Later he says, "His name, through faith in his name, hath made this man strong." Peter recognized and used the authority and power he had been given in Jesus' name.

KNOWING THE NAME

So how far have we come? We've seen that someone's name refers to their identity, character, reputation (their brand), and authority. Our name automatically carries with it all of the above—everything we have said, done, or failed to do; our power or impotence, and even the perception of what is in our heart and at our core. These are intricately connected and usually won't be perceived separately, although in common usage the word "name" can refer to each aspect separately, as we are about to see.

So let's *use* what we've learned. Equipped with the knowledge of *what's in a name*, we may read these verses about God like this:

Psalm 9:10 "They that know thy name *(identity, character, reputation and authority which includes his power)*, will put their trust in thee."

Psalm 76:1 "In Judah God is known: his name *(reputation)* is Great in Israel."

1 Samuel 17:45 "I come to you in the name *(authority and power)* of the Lord of Hosts, the God of the armies of Israel, whom thou hast defied."

John 17:6 "I have manifested (made to be seen) thy name, *(character, authority and power)* unto the men which thou gavest me out of the world."

Mark 16:17 "In my name *(authority and power)* they shall cast our devils."

In many other Bible verses that refer to the name of the Lord, we could insert the words character, reputation and/or authority to clarify the meaning intended. For example, God's character and reputation are indeed excellent, exalted, enduring, and worthy, and his authority exalted and enduring forever, as seen in these verses:

- Psalm 8:1 Excellent is thy name in all the earth.
- Psalm 148:13 His name alone is excellent.
- Isaiah 12:4 His name is exalted.
- Psalm 72:17 His name shall endure forever.
- James 2:7 His name is worthy.

In these next verses, which describe our proper response to his name, we could replace the word "name" with "character and reputation" and neither change the meaning of the word nor destroy the understanding. As an exercise, in these next verses think about which of the aspects of a name fit the context. (For example, we should trust his character; believe in his reputation, and fear, or reverence, his authority.)

We are told to:

- Know his name. Psalm 9:10
- Fear his name. Psalm 86:11
- Believe in his name. John 1:17
- Trust in his name. Psalm 33:21
- Praise his name. Psalm 113.1
- Remember his name. Psalm 20:7
- Call upon his name. Psalm 116:13
- Hold fast his name. Revelation 2:13

- Publish his name. Deuteronomy 32:3
- Declare his name. Psalm 22:22
- Make his name to be remembered. Psalm 45:17

Think of it! When we publish, remember, call upon, or believe in the name of the Lord, we're making known, remembering, believing in and calling upon his position, authority, power, and all of his reputation as known by his mighty acts. We're declaring, remembering, and trusting in his goodness and loving kindness, his holiness and justice, his wisdom and strength, and all of the other attributes of his character. (I should note here that in proclaiming the name of the Lord, we are proclaiming, as well, his revelatory names which we mentioned in Trail One. We should also know, trust, publish, believe, and hold fast to the names by which he revealed his covenant relationship with us.)

Now that we understand what's in a name, the "name of the Lord" is richer in meaning for us, and it will be easier to see which aspect of the name is being used in Psalm 138:2.

The chase continues on a nicely paved road.

Thinking about Chapter Three

SELF DISCOVERY QUESTIONS:

1. Do you know someone whose reputation is without flaw? What does this tell you of his/her character?
2. Have you ever made a decision specifically in order to preserve your reputation? Why did you do that?
3. What are the areas in which you have authority? Where does that authority come from?
4. Who has authority over you? Why is that authority there?

TRUTH CHASER'S PRAYER:

Dear God,
    You are my very own Father. Please help me make right choices so that my reputation will never bring shame to you. May my life bring honor to your name.

CHAPTER FOUR

Above All Thy Name

*"Suit the action to the word;
the word to the action."*

WILLIAM SHAKESPEARE
Hamlet

4.

"…for thou hast magnified thy word above all thy name."
~ Psalm 138:2

When I was a teacher of English grammar, sentence construction definitely took precedence over philosophy in my lesson plans. I still hoped, however, to establish in my students, whether in fourth grade or high school, a respect for words as carriers of knowledge and understanding.

Words *mean something*, and communicate specifically. When a word has several definitions, it is the *context* which tells us which specific meaning is applicable. In the next leg of the journey, we will be looking for the meaning of the word "name" which fits within the context of Psalm 138:2.

Recognizing several different ways of looking at the word, we need to put this passage under a microscope. This process may seem picky, but it is necessary if we are to understand what the psalmist is telling us.

Here we go:

Psalm 138:2 "I will worship toward thy holy temple, and praise thy name for thy loving kindness and thy truth: for thou hast magnified thy word above all thy name."

In this verse, the second "for" clearly indicates that the psalmist is praising God for something he has done. The passage is quite explicit about the fact the writer is praising God *because* of his treatment of his word—that he has magnified his word above all his name.

It would appear that this *magnification of God's word above His name* has shown the psalmist something of God's character that is praiseworthy—specifically, God's loving-kindness and truth. Therefore, whatever conclusion we come to about the meaning of "the magnified word," it must somehow show us these attributes of God's character.

If we don't understand what the psalmist is saying about the magnified word then, quite possibly, the part of God's character it reveals may also remain a mystery to us.

Well then, let's examine it. How can God magnify his word above all his name?

We recognize that in different contexts the word "name" can refer to any one or all of the different aspects of one's name. Now our challenge is to recognize which aspect is used in the context of Psalm 138:2.

Let's look at the passage in this way:

"Thou hast magnified (lifted up, exalted) your word above all your *identity*."
"Thou hast magnified (lifted up, exalted) your word above all your *character*."
"Thou hast magnified (lifted up, exalted) your word above all your *reputation*."

Is it making sense yet? In this context, it's difficult to understand how God could magnify his word above his identity, his character, or his reputation. If he could, what would be its significance? How would it reveal his truth and loving kindness? In this instance, could the correct use of the word "name" refer to God's authority?

Let's see how that application would sound in this sentence:

"Thou hast magnified (lifted up, exalted) your word above all your authority, *your right and power to rule.*"

Could God possibly exalt his word above his very right to rule? If he could, would this mean that when God has given his word on something, he won't ever allow his right to rule to overturn that word?

A better question might be: Would a God of truth and loving kindness do anything *but* elevate his word in that way?

Think about it. Shouldn't we all magnify our word above our right to do as we wish? Don't all people of integrity do that?

The quote at the beginning of this chapter is taken from a scene in Shakespeare's *Hamlet* where Hamlet is giving instructions to actors about how to act. It's not about integrity at all. But, really, shouldn't we all suit our actions to our words?

Sometimes, we don't. Sometimes our actions and our words don't resemble each other at all. I am reminded of a time some years back when, as thanks in response to a favor, some friends invited my husband and me to lunch at one of the finer restaurants in town. Naturally, we accepted the invitation and a date was set. On the day of our lunch date we received a call saying they would have to postpone. Something had come up; could we rebook? We did, of course. No problem.

Then it happened again about four or five times. We eventually became uncomfortable about the invitation and, I'm embarrassed to say, were making a mental note to avoid doing anything else for them that would result in their thanking us with an invitation to dine together.

We did finally do lunch together and had a very nice time with them. However, even though the episode involved something as inconsequential as lunch, and even though it was no doubt an isolated incident and in no way indicative of their normal behavior, for a while—and I'm not proud of this—it made a difference in how we viewed them. Their reputation suffered, even if just in our eyes.

It is epidemic in our society: We don't take our words seriously. Our actions show we are only halfheartedly committed to our words. We write "our word" in a contract and sign our name under it, symbolically upholding our word with our authority. Then we look for loopholes. In fact, most of us will readily admit we think of backing out of a commitment or a promise as being within our rights and not indicating any weakness of character. It just means we have changed our mind.

In case you've been thinking unkindly of the friends I just mentioned, remember that we live in a world where it is sometimes impossible to keep our word. Circumstances beyond our control can make it impossible for us to fulfill our verbal commitments or even our written contracts. In some cases, we may even have spoken the words in haste, not realizing that we couldn't fulfill them, and in others—yes, every now and then—something more important comes up.

For all these reasons and more, we accept the premise that we have the right to change our minds and, indeed, sometimes must do so. But, unfortunately, here's the problem, and here's the reason I mentioned that lunch story to begin with: We tend to think God does the same thing!

We think God—who sees and knows everything—will surely know if, or when, it's best not to fulfill something he said. We presume any lack of action on his part would be for our good because we know he loves us. We say, "After all, God is sovereign," and we expect that his sovereignty is working for our good, even if it appears his promises were not fulfilled.

But what do we mean when we say God is sovereign? Webster's New Dictionary says it is an adjective, meaning "supreme, possessing absolute authority within a given sphere." When used as a noun, it refers to the person who possesses that authority. A king is called the sovereign because he has acquired, by some means, the right to rule in a specific geographical area or over a specific people group.

When we refer to a country as a sovereign state, we're saying that the people and government of that country have the exclusive right to rule in that country.

Sovereignty, then, is absolute authority or right to rule.

If Psalm 138:2 is saying God elevates his word above his authority or right to rule, is it possible, therefore, that it is actually saying that *God has exalted his word above his sovereignty*—that his very sovereignty upholds his word?

That might not be a stretch for us, but what if it's also saying he will never overrule his word? Strange thought, perhaps, but let's consider it for a minute.

There is a verse in the New Testament that lets us know how God wants us to treat our words. It may give us a clue about what kind of value he puts on words. James 5:12 tells us to let our "yes" mean "yes" and our "no" mean "no." James wants us to mean (hold fast to) what we say and say what we mean (what we intend to hold fast to). Psalm 15:4 tells us to "swear to our own hurt and change not."

Now think about this: If God instructs us to have that regard for our words—as weak and foolish and unwise as we are—can he have less regard for, or commitment to, his own word?

Numbers 23:19 tells us that God is not a man that he should lie. Unlike us, God *can be* and *is* committed, firmly and irrevocably, to his word. That's why the Psalms can declare that God's word is forever settled in heaven. His word is not temporarily settled, merely until he has a better idea or until he gets more information or changes his mind on a whim. The psalmist says, "Forever, O Lord, thy word is settled in heaven" (Psalm 119:89).

Could God possibly have known when he spoke his promises that he would always, forever, be willing and able to fulfill them?

I'm pretty sure Jesus thought so. In his famous pre-ascension prayer, Jesus refers several times to God's words. In John 17:8 He says, "For I have given them the words which Thou gavest me," and again in verse 14, "I have given them Thy word."

Jesus had given his disciples lots of words—words about his purpose, about who he is and why he came, about their calling and how they were to live, and so much more. All of these words, according to Jesus, were what he heard his father saying.

Jesus obviously felt God's words would bear passing on to us and would stand throughout all time. And, obviously, that we *needed* them.

But think about it: Would God, who is all knowing, all powerful, and all wise—and who knows the end from the beginning—speak any words without absolute knowledge of their worth and of his willingness and ability to establish them all?

Of course not! Unlike us, he is not handicapped with ignorance, incompetence, or selfishness. When God spoke to any man, whether specifically to one man or to a nation or to mankind, he did so knowing his words were wise, good, fitting, and true. Always true; never overturned!

We can see why this knowledge about God—about his unchangeableness and *faithfulness to his word*—would cause the psalmist to praise his name for his loving kindness and truth.

Let's look at our springboard again.

Psalm 138:2 "I will worship toward thy holy temple, and praise thy name for thy loving kindness and for thy truth: for thou hast magnified thy word above all thy name."

Is it still difficult to get your mind around the thought that God's sovereignty will always uphold his word? If so, please don't dismiss the thought yet.

First of all, think of the implications.

Just think for a moment about God's actions "for his name sake." God was careful that his actions toward the children of Israel would be in line with words he had spoken—his promise to Abraham, Isaac, and Jacob that their children would be blessed.

Also, since he had sent Moses to deliver his people from the bondage of Egypt and expressed his intent before the heathen, he would not go back on his words and have his name—his reputation—polluted before them by destroying this stiff-necked and disobedient people.

Why do you suppose that was? Why would God make decisions and act "for his name sake"?

We saw in Psalm 78:7 why God wanted his reputation to remain intact. It was so that the generations to come "might set their hope in God, and not forget the works of God, but keep his commandments."

Surely, too, he wanted to ensure that whenever he spoke, he would be believed. He didn't just want to make his power known—he could bring the children of Israel out of bondage and into their promised land—but also his integrity. He wanted the children to know he would not abort the mission.

Without that knowledge what hope could survive?

God had great plans for his children, including us, but he knew that if they didn't believe him, they wouldn't hope in him. Without hope, they wouldn't walk in his ways, or obey him. If they didn't obey him, they could never be or do all that he wanted them to become and accomplish.

I learned a little about that particular aspect of human nature when I was teaching ten-year-olds. I found out very early on in my teaching career that I had better be very careful what I said to them. I learned that I should never promise anything I couldn't make good on, and if I wasn't absolutely sure I could carry out a particular promise, then I had better establish that fact up front.

Whenever my kids felt I couldn't be counted on, their frustration resulted in their becoming discouraged and distrustful. As a result, class control and a positive learning environment were affected adversely. If I ever lost my students' trust, I had to work very hard to win it back.

If it was so important that my students know my integrity, then surely it's just as important—even more so—that we, God's children, know his integrity.

And, surely, his faithfulness to uphold his word to the Israelites was not just for their sake. It was for our sake too. How would it change our lives if we expected God's sovereignty to uphold his word? Would it affect our relationship with God? Might it even affect the choices we make and the things we'll try to accomplish?

What we believe and know about God affects our choices. That's made clear in the verse from Daniel 11:32, "They that know their God shall be strong and do exploits." Again, in the words from Psalm 9:10, "They that know thy name will put their trust in thee."

Included in the knowledge of God's name is not just the knowledge of his power and authority. It is also the knowledge of his character as shown by his actions, specifically his integrity—that he does, indeed, exalt his word, giving it a place of prominence above his very name.

Think again about Abraham, David, and the three Hebrew children. Is it possible that their knowledge of God's integrity was the source of the confidence of our heroes of the faith?

If Abraham knew God's integrity, it might explain why he expected Isaac to return down that mountain with him. He would have reasoned that since God had said Abraham's progeny would spring from Isaac—and Isaac was not yet a father—then Isaac would have to continue to live in order to fulfill the word God had spoken. That's why Abraham believed Isaac would live even if he offered him as a sacrifice.

If David knew this about God, then perhaps that knowledge was the source of his confidence to stand before Goliath without a cringe. Maybe he was not merely presuming success based on his previous history.

It's clear that David carried more than presumption, five stones, and a sling into his battle. David carried confidence in God's promise that he would "cause thine enemies that rise up against thee to be smitten before thy face...and flee before thee seven ways." He believed his enemy would run away because that is what God had said would happen. He expected smitten enemies and that's what he got.

And then there are the three Hebrews. If Shadrach, Meshach, and Abednego knew the integrity of God, that would be why they could say "God can" and "God will" deliver.

They knew their covenant which said that if they feared God, angels would stand guard round about them to deliver them. Their reverential fear of God was obvious in their refusal to eat the king's meat and in their refusal to bow down to the gods of that land. They expected God to uphold his word.

All of these great exploit-doers knew God's name. They knew his power and authority, certainly; they also knew that both of these upheld his word. They knew his integrity and because of it they had a simple trust in God and great faith in his words.

But how might the stories have gone if they hadn't known?

What might have happened if Abraham, instead of saying, "We will return," said, "I will return," because he thought God had changed his mind about Isaac being the one from whom the promise of nations would spring?

What might have happened if David had thought he was going to Goliath in his own name—his own authority and power? What if he hadn't expected to be backed up by his covenant God that day on that field? Would he have gone at all?

What might have happened if the three Hebrew children really *had* said "God may not deliver, because you just never know what God will do"?

Conversely, what might happen if *we* believed that God would always back up his word? What if we expected God to do just what he said?

What if we knew that the very sovereignty of God would be the upholder of his word and the guarantee of its fulfillment? What would we do?

As Good As His Word

Knowing that someone is "as good as his word" brings a significant degree of comfort to a relationship. If having knowledge of a *human's* commitment to his word is reassuring, then, surely, knowing that God is committed to his word should be even more so.

However, it also presents serious questions. I know many of you right now are asking what has gone wrong when what God has promised—or expressed as being his will—hasn't come to pass.

Every day we see things that are opposite to what God calls good. All we have to do is watch the news or look around us. We probably don't even have to look far from home. I imagine almost every person reading this has some painful memories of circumstances or events that fit that description—the opposite of good.

I've been there and I'm convinced that God doesn't consider our questions to be evidence of lack of faith. He doesn't get angry with us or offended if we pray in frustration. He responds with kindness and mercy to every seeking heart—even the hurting ones. Like Job.

Job's Story

Job's story often brings comfort, as it should, to those experiencing times of loss and suffering. But to tell the truth, he used to present a huge problem for me.

When I was a child the only sermon I heard from the book of Job was based on the verse where he says, "Though God slay me, yet will I trust him." I was uneasy when I heard it, and confused. We sang "Jesus loves me, this I know" in Sunday school and it brought comfort and assurance. But then, in "big" church, I'd hear that God might want to slay me. That frightened me.

Later on, as a teenager, I thought, "Really, Job, could you possibly have made it more difficult for the rest of us?" His acceptance of death at the hand of one who loved him was a concept way out of reach for me.

Job was like a perfect older brother. I grew up the youngest of four girls, and that was tough enough. My three older sisters were spectacular and I often wished I could be more like them—Sylvia, the perfectionist; Emmie, the engaging, gregarious one; and Marilyn, the adventurer. The sisters definitely were hard acts to follow, but Job was worse. My sisters at least had the decency to have a few endearing flaws. Job didn't.

I really didn't like Job. I thought he was altogether too perfect—that is, until I finally read the book for myself.

When I read his story, I found out that even Job prayed a few frustrated prayers, like the ones in Chapter 10: "Shew me wherefore thou contendest with me." *What do you have against me, God?* And, "Wherefore hast thou brought me out of the womb?" *Why was I ever born?*

Doesn't it sound like Job was a bit of a truth chaser himself—albeit one who lived so circumspectly we might be excused for thinking he was pretty near perfect? Throughout much of his book we hear Job telling his friends he doesn't know why God has done these terrible things to him since he's always lived such a good life.

Job's three best friends, his infamous wrongly-named but would-be comforters, try to help him out by suggesting that he must have done evil or these things wouldn't have happened. Not very comforting, and Job doesn't buy it for a minute. Not too patiently he tells them they're wrong—that God obviously treats the righteous and unrighteous alike. After all, he is righteous and appears to have ended up with the same result justice would demand be reserved for the wicked.

But remember, in the book of Malachi God says he doesn't appreciate this kind of talk; it's called "stout against God.

Malachi 3:13,14 "Your words have been stout against me, saith the Lord. Yet ye say, What have we spoken so much against thee? Ye have said, It is vain to serve God: and what profit is it that we have kept his ordinance and walked mournfully before the Lord of hosts? And now we call the proud happy; yea, they that work iniquity are set up; yea, they that tempt God are even delivered."

So, obviously, God couldn't have been thrilled with this part of Job's speech.

On and on, the debate and the misery continues until Job's wife—maybe hoping to bring an end to his suffering—tells him to go ahead and curse God and die.

What a sad state! The only person who consistently makes good sense in the book and who doesn't get a rebuke from God for speaking "words without knowledge," is young Elihu.

Watching and listening, Elihu waits until all his elders have finished speaking and then—I paraphrase—basically says, "Job, get your eyes off yourself. Get them on God. See who he is." Then he goes on to give a wonderful description of God in Chapters 33 to 37.

You know the story. God finally speaks for himself. The end result is that Job turns to God, sees him as his redeemer and his help, and says, "I have heard of Thee with the hearing of the ear [perhaps implying misinformation], but now mine eye [accurate knowledge, at last!] seeth Thee." A wonderful end!

For me, one of the most comforting takeaways from Job's story is that even though Job spent much of the book justifying himself instead of God, God met him right where he was and brought him to a good end.

Maybe God knows that honest seekers of truth are, in fact, seeking him. And Job—whatever his flaws—was an honest seeker.

Nugget for Seekers from Job's Story

To seekers, I would give one nugget of wisdom in the words of Pastor Bill Johnson from Redding, California. Pastor Johnson says he refuses to let what he doesn't know interfere with what he does know—which may be part of what Job learned in the end.

For example, we may never know why specific tragedies happen. In fact, we shouldn't even try to judge why tragedies, troubles or failures happen to other people. Trying to understand the life issues of others may result in our judging people based on scriptures that were "meant for us to live by ourselves, and were never meant for us to judge others by"—as my wise daughter counseled me one day when I was quoting scripture to rant about a fellow Christian who had let me down.

Even worse, trying to understand someone else's circumstances may result in our deciding that perhaps sickness, abuse, tragedy and loss were part of God's good and loving plan for that person, no matter what his word says to the contrary.

The truth is we don't know someone else's walk with God. Remember, we are told to work out our own salvation with fear and trembling, not someone else's.

So, what are we to question and where are we to turn for answers? We all instinctively know there must be answers even if we think we'll only get them when we get to Heaven.

If we *are* to have answers here on earth, we have to go to the only truth that is absolute and unchanging.

That truth is found in scriptures that explain what God has said about himself, about us, and about his plans and purposes. Our beliefs have to be formed by these, not by any conclusions we might come to from what we see happening around us, or even to us.

The bottom line is this: when we're surrounded by mountains and giants, we would be wise to hold on to what God has already called truth—his word.

Thinking about Chapter Four

SELF DISCOVERY QUESTIONS:

1. Have you ever known someone you couldn't trust? Why couldn't you trust him/her?
2. Have you ever felt that God's sovereignty meant that he may not do what he says?
3. What circumstances or experiences have made you think this?
4. Are you willing to examine something you have always believed to be true, and see if it stands up to scrutiny?

TRUTH CHASER'S PRAYER:

My Father,

I have a lot of questions. This journey is not as easy as I thought it might be. Thank you that you will not let me lose my way as long as I stay close to you and listen to the voice of your word. I'm beginning to know your ways, dear Father, and trust you because I know your name.

CHAPTER FIVE

God's Good Name:
The Foundation for Trust and Faith

"Good name in man and woman, dear my lord,
Is the immediate jewel of their souls:
Who steals my purse steals trash;
'tis something, nothing;
'Twas mine, 'tis his,
and has been slave to thousands;
But he that filches from me my good name
Robs me of that which not enriches him
And makes me poor indeed."

WILLIAM SHAKESPEARE
Othello

5.

"A good name is rather to be chosen than great riches, and loving favor than silver and gold." ~ Proverbs 22:1

We started out looking at the ancient heroes of the faith because their lives modeled trust in God. Apparently, our heroes' knowledge of God's good name gave them such confidence in him that it resulted in their steely resolve to obey his commandments, even to putting their very lives and all they loved on the line in the face of apparently ridiculous odds.

One reason we have had trouble relating to that kind of "extreme" trust—beside the fact that we haven't thought on his name very much—is that we commonly use the words trust and faith as if they mean the same thing. We need to understand how the words "trust" and "faith" are used in Biblical context. In that context, although they are connected, they are not the same.

TRUST

Trust is based on knowledge. The Bible says so. We saw it earlier:

Psalm 9:10 "They that know thy name will put their trust in thee."

Psalm 9:10 confirms that our ability to trust someone, even God, is directly related to what we know of that person's character. In fact, knowledge of someone's good name is the only basis for real trust.

Sometimes we're asked to trust someone whose actions don't portray trustworthiness. For any number of reasons we may feel obligated to trust in these cases and so we decide to do so, sometimes to our detriment.

Many of us think that trusting others says something good about our own character. We don't like to think of ourselves as distrustful so we try to give trust as a gift. But even though our will is involved in trusting, as it is in everything else we do, deciding to trust where there is no basis for it—that is, little or no evidence of good character—is effectively gambling. Sometimes, because we love someone or because we need to, we decide to gamble and we call it trust. But real trust is based on knowledge.

So then, what do we know about God that should make us trust him? God is good and merciful; God is faithful and kind; God is loving and gracious. All reasons to trust him.

We also know that God is sovereign. We saw earlier that Psalm 24: says, "The earth is the Lord's and the fullness thereof; the world and they that dwell therein," and he, therefore, has authority over what is his. He has the right to rule all his creation.

And there's the rub!

Tradition has told us that because God is sovereign, all that happens in this world has received his approval. Many of us, confused by the discrepancy between what we see around us and what we read in the Bible, get some degree of comfort from the thought, "God is in control,"—because a sovereign God, we think, would definitely be in control of everything.

Because we know God is good, we assume that the tragic things that occur do so for a good reason. We suppose the sickness, poverty, abuse, and death must have some measure of good, if God allowed it, because we trust that God will do right.

However, if actions create reputation, and they do, then someone responsible for—or even approving of—everything that happens on this earth will develop quite a reputation. If we believe that all we see happening around us has passed through God's administrative desk, then his reputation will be adversely affected.

Needing comfort and assurance that all is well, we read books that are intended to help us be at peace with a God who doesn't seem to do what his own word would lead us to expect of him. These well-intentioned authors basically tell us to trust God's love and wisdom. In other words, trust in the character of God, accept whatever happens as being his will for us for some unfathomable good purpose, and learn to embrace the process—the wild adventure.

Because we know in our hearts we should be able to trust God, and because we desperately want to overcome—even if just emotionally—the troubles that hound us, we do what they say and try to trust.

We try, but soon we have difficulty putting shoes on that kind of trust. How do we walk it out? What, specifically, does that trust give us to walk toward?

More importantly, what does it cause us to do with what God said in his word, even if we do manage to attain a measure of peace with the God the authors describe? Our attempt to trust must never cause us to set aside what God has said, but often the kind of trust these authors suggest makes us do just that.

Here's the problem: we can't please God if our attempt to trust causes us to let go of even one word he has spoken because, according to the Apostle Paul, the words God has spoken are the source of our faith.

FAITH

Where do we get faith?
Romans 10:17 says "faith cometh by hearing, and hearing by the word of God."

Why is it important?
Hebrews 11:6 tells us "Without faith, it is impossible to please God."

What is its purpose?
Hebrews 10:38 makes it clear that "the just shall *live* by faith."

Isn't it interesting the Bible doesn't say the just shall live by trust? It says the just shall live by faith. Remember, trust is based on what we know of character. Faith, on the other hand, according to Romans 10:17, is based on words. While trust is the foundation for faith—in fact, there will be no faith without it—trust alone is not complete without faith. If we think about our own relationships we will see how that works.

I know a few good men and women. They are people of good character and I trust them without reservation. Not only are they good people; they also love me, and I am very confident they will never intentionally do anything to harm me. I trust they would only ever have good plans for me.

However, even though some of them might have the means, or the power, to pay off any debts I might have, I can have no faith that they will do that. I know their goodness, integrity, love, and power; and, yes, I trust them, but I don't have faith that they will pay my debts. Why not? Because they have never said they would.

However, if they ever *said* they would, I could and would have faith that they would do it because I know their integrity and can trust them because of it.

Faith would come by hearing their words, just as trust came by knowing their character.

In the same way, we may know God is good, loving and kind, and that God is sovereign—that he has all the authority and power to rule—but we can have no real expectation of any specific action on our behalf, no hope of any salvation, unless he has said something to that effect.

For example, we may be aware of God's love and mercy, but we still could never have faith for the new birth if he hadn't said it was available to all who would believe. Neither could we have faith for that salvation if we didn't *know* what he said about it.

That is the reason for the Great Commission: "Go ye into all the world and preach the gospel." Apparently, knowledge of the promise of salvation is crucial to its fulfillment in one's life.

In the same way, knowledge of the other promises of God is crucial to their fulfillment in our lives.

For example, if we know God is good, we'll trust in his goodness. But if we are convinced of his integrity and read that "by the stripes of Jesus" we were healed, then we can have faith in that word, and hope for it to be fulfilled.

Similarly, if we experience lack and know that God says he'll be our provider, then we can have faith in that word and have real, firmly based hope for the future.

And if we feel lost in life and read that God will give wisdom to those who ask unwaveringly, we will take courage and expect that God will direct our paths.

Eventually, real trust will give birth to the kind of faith that holds fast to the words of the trusted one.

Real faith holds fast. It has to. For some reason, it seems, in the justice system of the universe, faith must be tested. Therefore, like the heroes of the faith we looked at earlier, we sometimes have to hold fast to God's words in the face of some very contrary circumstances.

In our examples of Abraham, David, and the three Hebrews, we see they held fast to God's words in severely trying times. Apparently, not one of them thought him unpredictable. They considered him to be absolutely trustworthy and his word a secure, unmovable foundation for their faith. They didn't say, "God I trust you. Therefore, I won't expect you to keep your word in this instance." Not once.

Their knowledge of God's character enabled them to believe and act on his word, and that word was established, not only for them, but also for many others around them.

REASONABLE FAITH

Does that kind of faith seem unattainable—or unrealistic and unreasonable?

I'm not suggesting for a moment that it was easy for these men, or that they didn't ever waver or lose courage. They probably did. Even though the Bible doesn't tell us this, I can imagine Abraham walking up that mountain fighting thoughts of taking his son and running.

But Abraham knew God, and even though there may have been horrible pictures assaulting his mind of what was ahead, he must have been too convinced of God's faithfulness to his word to run away from his command. He probably didn't know exactly what God was up to or why this command was given, but he had already walked with God for many years and he knew God kept his word. God's faithfulness was what he trusted in as he climbed his mountain.

Maybe, when the three young Hebrews smelled the smoke from the furnace, they had to encourage each other in the promises that were the basis of the hope they expressed in "our God can and will…" As they felt the heat of the flames, they might have struggled to hold on to the confidence in God that birthed their resolve not to bow to a false god. We aren't told they did, but it's possible.

Then there's David. Actually, we really don't get any sense of David wavering in front of Goliath. I'm pretty sure it didn't occur to him to hide behind a bush that day and whimper, "Oh dear God, what have I done?"

Although we might be tempted to put that down—as his elder brother probably did—to the arrogance of youth, we have to remember that David had already seen God keep his promise to deliver him from his enemies. He had already seen the lion and the bear bite the dust, so he knew God was faithful. His confidence wasn't presumptive. History shows it wasn't misplaced.

These are amazing stories. Yet, all of these heroes were unmistakably human, just like us. In fact, Abraham and David, whose lives we follow longer than the three Hebrews, are often found to be struggling in their faith and going back to God with questions and, sometimes, repentance. Occasionally, just like us, they had to be picked up and helped out of the messes they made.

In the end, however, all of them spoke and acted in ways that show us they firmly put their faith in God's promises, and trusted and obeyed his directions—even though at times their threatening circumstances made their faith look unreasonable and foolish and maybe even blind.

But real faith is never blind; real faith sees.

Faith sees the faithfulness of the One who spoke the words from which faith came.

Faith sees what was promised and experiences real peace and joy about it before it is seen by natural eyes.

Faith often may *feel* blind, however, because of all the things we can't see and don't know. Here's an illustration of that:

The school where I taught in Texas had a beautiful new campus just outside of town. Because there were no street lights, it was very dark out there at night. The grounds just behind the playground were very rough and uneven and there were felled trees, small creeks, and other dangers to one who might be walking in the dark of night without a light.

If, however, while trying to make my way through that dark place, I had someone who could see the way and could tell me where to go, I could walk safely in the dark by faith in the words of that person.

Jesus said his sheep hear his voice and they won't follow the voice of a stranger, but I've learned we need to cultivate our listening skills.

Most of the time, the words we listen to will be those passed down to us in the Bible. In fact, reading his written word as if it is written to us personally and with a heart to obey is what sharpens our listening skills. His voice then is more recognizable when we hear it as the still small voice of the Spirit in our heart—the unbidden thought that we know didn't come from our own intellect and that is always in agreement with the principles laid down in his written word.

This next story illustrates what I'm trying to say. When our family moved to Texas, part of our funding was a forgivable loan from the university where my husband had been teaching. We were told we would have to pay taxes on the full amount of the loan when it was forgiven. While we were still in Texas, I started praying about the tax money we were going to need when we returned home. We didn't have it right then, and I knew we wouldn't have time to save that amount before it became due.

One day as I was praying I heard in my heart, "That's taken care of. You won't have to pay those taxes." Later I told my husband, "I don't think we're going to have to pay taxes on that income," and told him why.

Being the ever-practical business professor, he reminded me of a fact of Canadian life: If you receive income, you pay taxes—unless, of course, you have enough money to find "shelter" somewhere. He did agree that we could trust God to meet our need and provide the money when we needed it. That was good enough for me, so I left it alone and didn't revisit the possibility that we wouldn't have to pay taxes.

When we came back to Canada and received that gigantic—it looked that way to me, at least!—tax bill, I got to praying. As I had learned to do by now, I reminded God of what he had said in his word about meeting our needs, thanked him for his willingness to do it, and let him know I was holding fast to his word.

I was shocked when I heard again: "I told you it was taken care of. You won't have to pay those taxes. Be thankful for that." Not those words exactly, but the clear impression of that fact.

I told my husband. A wise and, therefore, cautious man, he decided his next step would be to go to Revenue Canada to see what method of payment they might suggest since at this point—no matter what I had heard—we still owed them money.

Revenue Canada, predictably, didn't care that we had no money and suggested a bank loan. Somewhat discouraged, Glenn went back to his office where he found this note on his desk: "Glenn, I overheard you talking about your tax bill and I thought you might be interested in this."

Attached to this note from a fellow professor—a tax lawyer— Glenn found a release from The Canadian Taxpayer regarding the non-taxability of monies given to employees for the purpose of higher education. The reform it described was in response to a court case involving an employer who felt his employee shouldn't have to pay the tax on such a monetary benefit. The court case was undertaken in the same year that I first heard that small voice in Texas.

That note and its happy attachment made a believer out of my husband. There's a lot more to this story, but we held on to that word from God for two more years, and—even though for all that time no one but us agreed with what God said—in the end we were able to do a happy dance in our kitchen when we finally held in our hands the tax bill with a lovely zero on the bottom line.

We didn't have to pay the tax.

God has ways that we know nothing about. He just wants us to believe what he says, and act accordingly. Didn't Jesus say, "Blessed are those who have not seen [with the natural eye] and yet believe"?

Abraham didn't yet see Isaac raised, but believed and climbed a mountain to sacrifice his only son.

David didn't yet see Goliath smitten, but believed and ran to a giant with stones in a sling.

The three Hebrew children didn't yet see their delivering angel, but believed, refused to bow, and walked into the flames.

And out of the abundance of God's word in their hearts, their mouths spoke:

"The lad and I will return."

"This day I will smite thee!"

"Our God can and will deliver us from your hand, O King!"

From their example we see that faith is believing and acting on the words of someone whose integrity we know and whose character is worthy of trust—even when we can't see one step ahead of us. When all we can see is his faithfulness.

INTEGRITY

We talked about it in Chapter Four, but it bears further attention here: Integrity is the element of character which provides the surest foundation for trust and faith.

In someone who has integrity there is wholeness. That person's thoughts, words, and actions will be of the same "stuff." From what we have seen of our Bible heroes we can tell they all must have been assured of God's integrity—that his thoughts, words, and actions would all look the same. We need to be assured of it too.

It is an absolute fact we will never have faith in, or hold fast to, the words of someone whose character we perceive to be flawed, no matter how much we try. Even if the perception is incorrect or subconscious, it will cripple our trust and weaken our faith.

I imagine we all can think of someone, maybe even someone we love dearly, whose word doesn't seem to be his bond. It may be a father who said yes to a request just to get some peace and quiet from persistent nagging, but without any intent to follow through. It may be a teacher who promised some special favor but backed out when it became too difficult to do, or a husband or wife who didn't fulfill a promise because, after all, it just couldn't be helped.

We do try to understand when that happens, and most of us are very forgiving, especially to those we love. But after a while—if it happens too often—we really don't have a lot of faith in what they say.

Just so, in spite of the love we have for God, if we really don't think his word is his bond we won't rely too heavily on what he says.

Sadly, because we attribute to him the responsibility for the terrible situations we see around us, and because those situations are not what his word describes as his will for us, we are often unsure of his faithfulness to fulfill his words, even though we believe him to be loving and wise.

If we reach that point, our confidence in his integrity has been crushed.

Tragically, when that happens—even though we have an unshakeable belief in our salvation and a firm expectation of eternal life in Heaven—*our reality* is that we live our lives on earth as though God has spoken no other promise than eternal life through faith in Jesus, and perhaps comfort through our pain.

Some of us don't even expect that much.

The reason for this is as simple as it is clear: We won't hold fast to any of his words that we aren't sure he holds fast to as well. We may think we should and we may try to, but we won't.

I wonder if that's why we sometimes don't find the time to read the Bible, or if when we do it's merely so we can feel good that we have checked off a duty and, hopefully, have pleased God by doing so. Perhaps we don't really consider the Bible relevant to our everyday lives since we can't count on it. As a result, we go on living wordlessly.

But, surely, we can know God upholds his word!

In *The Voyage of the Dawn Treader,* the fifth book in C.S. Lewis' *Chronicles of Narnia,* Aslan the Lion—who many literary critics suggest represents Jesus—delivers a great line to Lucy when he appears to her in response to her use of the Magician's book.

When Aslan tells her he came because of what she did, she won't believe it because she thinks her actions couldn't possibly affect a response from the great Aslan. She says, "As if anything I could do would make you visible!"

Aslan replies, "It did. Do you think I wouldn't obey my own rules?" (159)

What a picture of God's integrity!

The Currency Of The Kingdom

My father, an avid reader and lover of the Bible, once told me, "I'm starting to believe that faith is the currency of the kingdom." I think he may have been right.

Somehow, in the legal system of Heaven and this universe, belief is a necessity—not only belief in God's existence, but also belief in his words.

In Isaiah 7:9, the prophet Isaiah had been sent with a message from God to Ahaz. It was good news: His enemies' plans would not come to pass. But God also told Ahaz, "If ye will not believe, surely you will not be established."

Believe what?

Believe the message Isaiah had brought! Even though God had spoken what was to be, Ahaz had to believe it in order for it to be established.

God, who had all the authority and all the power needed to manifest his promise, was saying, "Ahaz, if you don't accept my words, it will be to you as if I didn't say them."

I know it seems incredible. We are, after all, talking about one who is truly sovereign. Surely, you may say, God's words don't need man's acceptance in order for them to come to pass.

I'm inclined to agree.

But they do when he says they do.

We see the truth of that repeated too often when people reject the gospel. God has sent us his word in John 3:16. It says that because he loved us he sent his son, Jesus, to carry the sins of the whole world and pay the wages sin required. It doesn't say he *will* put our sins on Jesus. It says he has already done so. Yet, if people don't accept God's words, it is *to them* as if he said nothing.

A savior has provided salvation for every man and woman born on this earth, and yet, if they don't believe, it will be *to them* as if nothing has been done.

The life-giver came, but if he's rejected, death prevails.

Light came, but if that light is rejected, darkness prevails.

It remains, for some, as if Jesus did nothing.

Not God's choice; not his plan.

In the same way, if we, as Christians, let go of any promise God has made, it will be *to us* as if the words had never been spoken.

Ephesians 2:12 speaks indirectly to this issue when it says: "At that time ye were without Christ, being aliens from the commonwealth of Israel, and strangers from the covenants of promise, having no hope and without God in this world."

When Ephesians refers to being strangers from the covenants of promise as being without hope and without God in the world, even though it refers to the time before the promise came to Gentiles, we can infer that if we, as Christians, live without the promises we are living *practically* godless lives.

This truth is tragic: If we believe that God's sovereignty trumps his promises, we will, of necessity, live life in much the same way as strangers from the covenants of promise, even though we are blood-bought, church-going, Bible-reading children of God.

We will, then, think that the faith of the Bible heroes is unattainable and maybe even rather ridiculous.

Throughout the Bible, we see our Father trying to get across to us the necessity of believing his words, even if that belief looks unreasonable. I say "looks unreasonable" because it's never unreasonable to have faith in God. It's unreasonable not to.

A Light In A Dark Place

We live in a dark place, as dark as that school yard in Texas I told you about. Psalm 23 tells us that though we walk through the "valley of the shadow of death" we need fear no evil. That valley is life on this earth. From the time we enter this earth as tiny vulnerable babies until the day we leave, we're shadowed by the dark presence of death.

That presence has been here almost since the beginning. In this bright and beautiful home God created for his family, where Adam walked clothed in glory, there was a tragic day when the light went out.

On that horrible day, when Adam chose to act on the words of the rebellious angel Lucifer, he effectively became Lucifer's servant and put God's enemy in charge on this earth, and the sovereign God—because he is righteous—had to honor his action. The glory left and Adam, horrified, realized he was naked and vulnerable.

We may not be able to imagine what it was like for Adam and Eve to live in glory, but we do know that on the day the glory left, death began its reign of terror and we all know how it feels to live in its shadow. We have lived with it ever since and I dare say every fear we have can be traced back to our fear of death.

Why does Psalm 23 tell us that, even on this earth where death and darkness must be allowed to remain for a time, we need not fear?

It's because "Thou art with me."

Adam's sovereign and righteous God had provided a remedy: The light himself is with us.

There are actually two representations of light found in the Bible.

The first is Jesus. Isaiah, prophesying about Jesus' birth, said in Isaiah 9:2, "The people that walked in darkness have seen a great *light*: they that dwell in the land of the shadow of death, upon them hath the *light* shined."

Jesus, himself, said in John 8:12, "I am the *light* of the world; he that follows me will not walk in darkness."

Zacharias, John the Baptist's father, speaking of Jesus' coming, said, as recorded in the book of Luke, "The dayspring from on high hath visited us, to give *light* to them that sit in darkness and in the shadow of death, to guide our feet into the way of peace" (Luke 1:78, 79).

The second representation of light is God's word. In Psalm 119:105, the psalmist says, "Thy word is a lamp unto my feet and a *light* unto my path." Later in the same psalm he says, "…the entrance of thy words gives *light*; it gives understanding unto the simple."

How connected these two are!

How else do we follow Jesus, the light, if it is not by receiving, believing, and walking by faith in his words? If we don't, or if we can't because we don't know God's integrity, we still walk in some measure of darkness.

Certainly, God's word can only become a lamp and light to us when we believe it. It will only benefit us when we act on it.

Interestingly, the scriptures also tell us that we *live* by two things: God's word and faith. Jesus said man shall not live by bread alone but by every word that proceeds from the mouth of God. We saw in Hebrews that the just shall live by faith.

As they say in Texas, these two—faith and the word—are tied together with a very short rope!

We read earlier that without faith it is impossible to please God. Have you ever wondered why that is? There may be many reasons for it, but one seems obvious. If it is, indeed, by faith that we receive his promises fulfilled, we can see why it's impossible that he be pleased with less than that.

Thinking about Chapter Five

SELF DISCOVERY QUESTIONS:

1. Do you think God has a good reputation? Why? Why not?
2. Can you trust him? Why? Why not?
3. Can you have faith in what he says? Why? Why not?
4. If the answers to the above were negative, are you willing to change your opinion?

TRUTH CHASER'S PRAYER:

Dear Father,
I am willing to see my own heart. I am willing to change in any way that pleases you. Tell me if I have not believed something you have said.

PART TWO:
The Road Ahead

CHAPTER SIX

Lessons From Sunday School And Turtles

"The light of the body is the eye:
therefore when thy eye is single,
thy whole body also is full of light."

JESUS
Luke 11:34

6.

The Parable Of The Oklahoma Turtle

A few years ago, early on a quiet spring morning, I was driving home from Tulsa, Oklahoma, with my daughter who had just graduated from university. We were the only car on a long stretch of highway. Gillian was sleeping and I was enjoying the beautiful Oklahoma countryside when I saw what looked like a rock in the middle of the road. I kept my eyes on it, wondering what it was, and as I got closer I saw it was a turtle making its way across the highway. I was thinking "Oh, how cute! It's a…," when I felt a horrible bump. Tragically for that little guy, I went right where my eyes were looking!

That story reminds me of a chorus we sang in the little country Sunday school I attended as a child. It went like this:

"Oh, be careful little eyes what you see
Oh, be careful little eyes what you see.
For the father up above is looking down in love,
Oh, be careful little eyes what you see."

At the time, in Sunday school, I thought the song was about not displeasing God with what I looked at. But since my Oklahoma turtle encounter, I think the reason for its message might be this: We really do tend to go where our eyes are looking.

Every day we naturally look straight ahead when we walk. It's easy enough to recognize the difficulty of walking, and the danger, if we can't see where we are going. Our physical eyes are so important the very idea of living without them is horrifying.

As well as our physical eyes, we have another form of sight. We sometimes call it our mind's eye. The Bible calls it the eyes of our heart.

As we are meditating, or thinking, we are actually mentally seeing something. Just as we look toward where we want to walk, so we can and must deliberately place our mind's eye on where we know God has provided for us to go. We do that by thinking about those good things mentioned in Philippians 4:8.

Meditation on God's love, God's word, and God's right and power and faithfulness to perform his word, will bring a resurgence of hope for the "goodness of God to be seen in the land of the living."

On the other hand, meditation on the Goliaths of life—and the reasons for our own weakness or inadequacies—will deplete our expectation of God's involvement in our battles and possibly annihilate our courage to fight.

Remember our story about Abraham? He didn't spend his time wondering why God had asked him to sacrifice Isaac or worrying about his own inadequacy to produce another son. Even though he must have had the same emotions any father would have at such a request, Abraham kept his inner eyes on "in Isaac shall thy seed be called."

We don't hear David talking about Goliath's size or complaining about the apparent cowardice of the rest of the people of covenant. He kept seeing "The Lord shall cause thine enemies to be smitten before thy face."

And there's no record of Shadrach saying to Meshach and Abednego, "What went wrong? Why are we heading to certain destruction? Does God want to deliver us from slavery this way, by this terrible death?" They kept seeing the words written over one hundred years before, "Thou shalt not be burned."

From the record we are given, we can see they all kept their focus on the covenant word of their God and his faithfulness to establish that word.

The Eyes Have It

Our family has traveled and lived in several different cities because of my husband's career. This lifestyle brought with it the opportunity to see, up close, many local churches. It's always easy to see the beauty of Jesus in every one of these churches. It's sometimes just as easy to see how we lose our way.

At one time we attended a church where the statement of faith would include divine healing, the indwelling of the Holy Spirit, and God's provision for his people. However, the pastor—with the best of intentions, I'm sure—spent a lot of time preaching about why much of the church is sick, powerless, and poor.

It wasn't surprising that there was a pervasive atmosphere of sadness in the church. They looked too long on failure.

We need to be realistic and accurate in our assessment of any situation, but our focus must remain on God, not on ourselves or people around us.

This observation of another church gives an example of the danger of looking too much at our own efforts. At times, when it seemed—to me, at least—that the people were already unified in expression of praise and worship, I noticed that the leader would exhort the congregation, reminding them that there were higher heights yet to be attained in worship. This exhortation always resulted in louder praise which would last for just a minute or two. Then, as if tired by the exercise, everyone would shut down, and the spirit of worship that had earlier pervaded the atmosphere simply disappeared.

I noticed this happened often, so I began to watch for it. Sure enough, it happened every time: praise, interruption, shut-down.

For a while I puzzled over it. I knew these people. They weren't a rebellious group, so why wouldn't they follow through on the leader's instructions? I finally concluded, rightly or wrongly, that the reason for this phenomenon was their change of focus.

Perhaps before the exhortation the eyes—or thoughts—of the congregation were on God. Maybe afterward they focused, instead, on their performance.

Whether or not my assessment was accurate, there will be no argument that true worship can only flow from one whose eyes are on God.

All that—the turtle and the churches—just to say this: In the same way, true faith can only be released when our eyes are on God and his strength and faithfulness.

It is interesting that in the story of Job it was after Elihu's admonition that Job should get his eyes off himself and onto God that God showed up and turned Job's captivity.

In the previous examples of Abraham, David, and the three Hebrew children, we saw that no matter what was going on around them they kept their eyes on God's promise and his right, ability, and willingness to perform what he had said.

Another personal story illustrates this truth. When we were in Texas, while my husband was a doctoral student and making very little money, I was teaching in a private Christian school. My job was a great blessing since it provided not only funds desperately needed to keep body and soul together, but it also provided meaningful work and beautiful friends.

Unfortunately, it didn't provide pay during the summer months when school was out and, because I was an alien in that country, I couldn't just go get a job anywhere. In accordance with immigration rules, my work had to be in my profession and my would-be employer would have to go through months of paperwork and red tape to get me approved. For someone to do that for a few months was unreasonable, even if I had been allowed to work at something outside my field for a couple of months.

The result of all this was that, for the summer months, my budget was short about $800.00 each month. Perhaps not a lot of money—except when you don't have it!

For the first time in my life, it looked as if I would have to choose between eating and paying the rent. No matter how I looked at it, I couldn't figure out how to come up with the cash—short of begging, that is. I had never done that before; it seemed downright unbecoming to a Christian, and, besides, who knew if it would work?

In all my meditating on our predicament, my only hope came from the Bible—specifically the book of Philippians.

Philippians 4:6,7 says, "Be careful (full of care, my paraphrase) for nothing; but in everything by prayer and supplications, with thanksgiving, let your requests be made known to God, and the peace of God, which passeth all understanding (which is not based on what you can see and know, my paraphrase) shall keep your hearts and minds through Jesus Christ." And Verse 19 was my lifeline: "My God shall supply all your need according to his riches in glory by Christ Jesus."

In order to maintain my sanity, I kept that word before my eyes. I would like to say I didn't give another thought to my husband's and my inability to provide for our family, but it wouldn't be true. I thought about it all too often because I'm a bean counter at heart. I love to manipulate numbers but, no matter how much I tried, my numbers would not be manipulated with any happy result.

Thankfully, every time I went down that road and came to the same dead end I would remember what God had said. I knew that had to be my bottom line.

I had already learned, long ago, that he would back up what he said, so I reminded myself—over and over if I had to—that I could believe him, even though, right at that moment, I couldn't see where on earth the money would come from.

And provide he did—eight hundred extra dollars each month.

The first month's extra funds came as a result of a car accident I had been involved in when someone on the university parking lot backed out of his spot and into the side of our car as I was driving by. I was shaken up, but as I got out of my car I remembered something the apostle Paul said. So I said out loud, "This will turn for my good!"

When the other driver's insurance company interviewed me, I told them I was unharmed by the incident and that I had received an estimate of $400 for cost of repairs to my car. The interviewer asked, "So then, will $1100 be enough?"

Thinking that American insurance companies were considerably more generous than their Canadian counterparts, I agreed that the amount would cover things nicely and a few days later I had their check.

When we told a friend at church about our good fortune, not only was he surprised at the amount the insurance company had allowed us, he also said, "It shouldn't cost $400 to fix your car. I'll take you to my guy. He'll take care of you for much less than that."

True to his word, he did, and his friend did "take care of us" for much less. We came away from the whole transaction with—you guessed it—an extra $800, just what we needed for the first month of summer vacation.

I won't bog you down with the details of the following two months because there are lots of them, including overbooked hotels that paid for accommodations elsewhere, universities that gave overly generous honorariums, and three days' work turning into a few hours' effort. It's enough to say God has his ways. He kept his word in ways that I couldn't have imagined. And because of his grace and goodness, we had $800 over and above our regular income each month of the summer and on into the first month I was back at school.

Would that have happened if we hadn't kept our eyes on what God said about being our provider? We'll probably never know for sure but I tend to think not. I do know one thing: I would have had no peace at all. There's more about that in the next chapter, but why should we care to find out what would happen if we left God out of life's equation?

In the book of Hebrews, Chapter 12, the apostle Paul tells us how *not* to do that— how *not* to leave God out. He writes to some people who appear to be having a crisis of faith. He chastens them a little because, he says, they should have been teachers by now but he has to teach them again who Jesus is and what he did for them.

At the end of the book, he gives them some advice about how to keep the faith and run their race with patience: Look unto Jesus, the author and finisher of our faith.

When I was a teenager, we sang a chorus in church that went like this:

"Turn your eyes upon Jesus.
Look full in his wonderful face.
And the things of earth will grow strangely dim
in the light of his glory and grace."

This song isn't claiming that earthly things aren't important to God. Many things of earth are very important to God, especially those things that are part of our fulfilling our destiny.

It's saying that when we keep our inner eyes on Jesus, when we see his goodness, wisdom, and power, and when we know his favor and eagerness to show himself strong on our behalf, then the things of earth such as the giants and the mountains—and the lack of $800 a month—will be put in proper perspective. We'll see them as small in the light of his glory.

Ah, his glory! His love and mercy, goodness and grace, integrity and faithfulness, justice and power!

Oh be careful, little eyes, what you see!

Thinking about Chapter Six

SELF DISCOVERY QUESTIONS:

1. Is there something you are looking at right now that you don't want to move toward?
2. Do you believe it's what God wants for you?
3. Are there any scriptures that might lead you to a different place?

TRUTH CHASER'S PRAYER:

Dear Jesus,

You are my shepherd. Help me to listen to the voice of your word and to hear your still small voice in my heart. Help me keep my eyes on you as I follow you. And, Jesus, please let me know when my eyes wander.

CHAPTER SEVEN

Out Of The Abundance Of Your Heart

"Be not deceived, God is not mocked;
for whatsoever a man soweth,
that shall he also reap"

PAUL THE APOSTLE
Galatians 6:7

7.

"In quietness and in confidence is your strength." ~ Isaiah 30:15

My father went to Heaven at the age of 90, early in the summer of 2003. For his home-going celebration, our family chose a bulletin with these words on the front: The Greatest Believers are the Most Patient Waiters. A successful farmer, my father knew how to sow seed, water the seed, nourish the seed, and patiently wait for the harvest he expected it to bring. He was a great believer in the power of seed.

Jesus referred to God's word as seed. As believers, we must know how to sow God's word in our heart, water it with praise and meditation, nourish it with obedience and wait patiently and expectantly for its fulfillment.

Hopefully, as we have turned the pages of this book, we have prepared our hearts to be good ground for that seed.

As we meditate on God's integrity, it will help make our hearts good soil for the seed of his word, breaking up any ground hardened by disappointment and failures and removing stones of fear and doubt. It will also help us hold fast to the promises of God with faith and patience as did Abraham, David, and the three Hebrew children, even in the midst of contrary circumstances.

Psalm 112:7 says the righteous man is not afraid of evil tidings because "his heart is fixed, trusting in God."

It's true that God calls our belief in him righteous, and we are legally and effectively *made* righteous by our faith in the blood of Jesus. But it's not our righteousness that makes us unafraid when bad news comes. It is God's righteousness that makes us unafraid.

It is the integrity of God that causes the "made-righteous" man's heart to become fixed. Because we know him, we trust him. Because we trust him, we believe what he says. Because we believe his promises, we are unafraid. We can have a fixed heart because of his fixed word.

I expect there is another positive result of knowing God's commitment to his word. It will give us the strength and courage to do his will—to go as Peter did, in his name, and make his great name known.

Remember Peter? He was the one who walked on water with Jesus simply because Jesus said, "Come"—notwithstanding the little incident later when he took his eyes off Jesus, put them on the storm raging around him, and began to sink until Jesus reached out and helped him.

Peter's the one, too, who lost courage and denied Jesus on the infamous day of Jesus' trial, and yet later said to a crippled man, "What I have I give thee. In the name of Jesus Christ of Nazareth, rise up and walk!"

Why did Peter believe he had something to give? It surely wasn't because of his stellar performance. Could it be that he finally learned to *simply believe what Jesus said*?

Peter must have believed the words recorded in Mark 16:17-18, where Jesus told his disciples what they, or "he that believeth," could do in his name. Peter believed that, in spite of his own failures, everything Jesus' name represents would back up his words to the cripple.

One morning, during the time I was writing this, I was praying for my family. My daughter, who was attending university in another city, had called me the day before and, during the conversation, told me that her sinuses and ears were blocked. Her hearing was affected and she was in a lot of pain.

While I was praying, Peter came to mind.

Earlier, I had been writing about when Peter said, "That name, through faith in that name, has made this man strong." Having focused for days on God's faithfulness to back up his word with his power, I was keenly aware that just as Jesus had delegated his own authority to Peter, he had, by his own words, delegated his authority to me. And, at that moment, I had the responsibility to use it. I felt sure his power would back up my legitimate use of his name.

I was convinced that the name, the character, authority, and power of Jesus would back up *my* words if, in the authority of *his* name which he said was mine to use, I would command my daughter's ears to open and the swelling to go down.

So, all alone in my front room, with morning sunshine pouring through the window, I did just that.

The next day, Gillian called. I asked how her ears were. She exclaimed, "It was so strange! Yesterday, at around 1:00 o'clock, my ears suddenly got hot, and they began to drain! The pain is gone and I can hear fine!"

I had been praying at 11:30 am, which was 1:00 p.m. in her city. That name, through faith in that name, had made her ears whole.

Has this kind of result always happened?

No; not at all.

But it happens more often when my eyes remain on God and his faithfulness to his word.

I wonder if that could be at least part of what Jesus was talking about when he said, as recorded in John15:7, "If ye abide in me and my words abide in you, ye shall ask what ye will and it shall be done unto you."

Sometimes we have to work to regain a place where the word abides in us because, in this life, there will always be something that comes to steal the word from our hearts.

For example, several years ago when I was diagnosed with breast cancer, I realized that I had been foolishly neglectful. I had felt a thickening in my breast a year earlier but had ignored it, convincing myself that it was my imagination. Then, when I was faced with a very serious disease, my shame over my neglect almost caused me to let go of what I knew was God's desire to be my help. My shame kept my eyes on me.

My dear friend and former pastor, Lorne Rostotski, told me, "This is threatening your life. Psalm 103:4 says that God redeems your life from destruction. Expect Him to do what He said."

In other words, it's your life, not just your health, that's in jeopardy, so start looking in the right direction. Look at God's promise to deliver your life from destruction.

Given the battle going on in my head, I knew he was right; that's where my focus had to be.

As I did what he said, and also focused on other words related to the circumstance I was in, the "abiding" of the word became stronger. I began to thank God for all the wonderful words he had spoken, for all the great things he had already done for me, for his often proven faithfulness and for his loving kindness and truth. Confidence in God began to overcome shame and the fear that accompanied it, and eventually removed them altogether. I actually had the audacity—or perhaps it was just confidence in one who loved me—to ask God to redeem, buy back, the time I had wasted. Then I thanked him for it before I saw it.

Shame said, "You don't deserve that," but Jesus said, "Ask what ye will."

After the surgery the oncologist told me, "You had a very well behaved tumor!"

Apparently—given the history of the disease in my body—the tumor would have been expected to be much more advanced.

With a very grateful heart I thanked God. I still do today. I was very thankful for what the doctors had done but more grateful that "the Lord taketh my part with them that help me" (Psalm 118:7).

Always give credit where credit is due.

But, you may ask, how does this work? How is it possible that what we meditate on makes a difference in the outcomes of our life? We can easily understand how our thoughts can affect our choices and therefore also affect the natural results we attain in many endeavors, but how does it work when our own power is not involved? How can what we believe make a difference to our outcome when God is the only one who is able to affect the outcome—when supernatural power is necessary?

Maybe it is just as my father said. Maybe faith really is the currency of the kingdom.

I do know this: There are hundreds and thousands of stories of God backing up his word with his power and authority, not just in Bible times but in our day as well. In all of these stories, we find some pretty ordinary people who have trust and faith in God and the courage to act on what he says.

These stories can be ours, yours and mine, but we have to do our own trusting and obeying. Sometimes, while we're doing that, we are also trying to figure out how or when God will fulfill what he's promised.

Big mistake! That's not our job. It's his.

Ours is one we can do. We can meditate on God's great name— on all that it means—and let it strengthen our faith and courage. That may seem small, but it's powerful, and it's a vital part of our destiny.

Romans 8:29 tells us, "For whom he did foreknow, he also did predestinate to be conformed to the image of his Son, that he might be the firstborn among many brethren." Think of that. What might it look like?

Jesus walked in faith and courageous obedience and completed what he was sent to do. It's our privilege to do the works *we* were sent to do and be conformed—in this way—to the image of Jesus.

Destined, *pre*destined, to be like Jesus! Stunning!

DESTINY

It always surprises me when people say their destiny is something over which they have no control. They think the plan for their lives is somehow set in stone and, good or evil, they just stumble upon it.

The truth is that even though God has a predestined plan for our salvation and exciting works for each of us to do, we have to choose to walk out his plan. We have been given free will, the authority to make our own choices. We have also been given the responsibility to use that authority wisely.

God doesn't set his good plan out there for us to stumble upon without volition, and neither does he spread it out for us to see as a whole and then choose or refuse. Instead, he gives us his word as a light to our path and says he'll never leave us, but will instruct us all the days of our lives.

There's a precious moment in C. S. Lewis' *The Voyage of the Dawn Treader* when Lucy pleads with Aslan, "Oh, Aslan! Will you tell us how to get into your country from our world?"

He gently replies, "I shall be telling you all the time."

All the time, day by day, God is telling us how to live in the light. We can choose, refuse, or maybe even just neglect to take him up on his offer of guidance and accept his words as truth. We can choose, refuse, or neglect to walk in light. There is always a choice.

We couldn't possibly have been created in the image of God and not been given the power to choose.

The concept of choice is intrinsic in any covenant. Throughout the history of God's covenants with mankind, there is evidence of him telling us we have to choose. In the Old Testament, which is about the destructive power of sin, the people of the covenant had to choose to walk in obedience to God's laws, and there were many. In Deuteronomy, when God gives the old covenant blessings and curses to his people he says, "See, I have set before thee this day life and good, and death and evil; therefore choose life" (Deuteronomy 30:15-20).

Years later, in a message to King Zedekiah—who had asked God what he should do in the face of the besieging Chaldeans and the advancing army of King Nebuchadnezzar of Babylon—Jeremiah gives him God's reply: Their enemies will be victorious over them, but if they leave the city and fall into the hands of the Chaldeans, they will live. If they stay in the city, they will die at the hands of the Babylonians.

Then he says, "Thus sayeth the Lord, Behold I set before you the way of life and the way of death" (Jeremiah 21:8).

They had to choose the way they would go, and their outcome would be based on their choice.

Still today, under a new covenant, our destiny waits on our choices.

The New Testament is about the life-giving power of the grace-gift of righteousness received through faith in Jesus. There's so much wrapped up in that gift that is the subject of other Biblical books, but John 1:1-5 says something about the working of the gift: "In the beginning was the Word, and the Word was with God, and the Word was God...In him was life; and the life was the light of men... and the light shines in the darkness."

Life and light are available.

Surely, you say, no right thinking person will deliberately choose darkness and death.

You are right, of course, but some choose darkness by default. Even as Christians—though we are children of another kingdom and no longer prisoners of darkness or death—because we still live in the dark valley we have to choose the abundant overcoming life God provides *on earth* in the same way Abraham, David, and the three Hebrew children did, by on purpose accepting God's word as light and truth and not letting it go.

The word is always involved in bringing about the full manifestation of life, the intended result of the gift of righteousness. We receive the gift of righteousness by faith, and we don't lose it. But we choose to walk every day, as beloved graced children, in the light that is lovingly provided by the gift-giver.

We choose it.

It may be daunting to think our choices are so important, but, in all of this, can you see the hope you and I have? God has planned and provided for our success, not our failure!

He loves us and comforts us in our failure, and picks us up when we fall, but he has planned and provided so that every one of our lives might reflect the glory of his great name. We all get to choose life.

But he won't make us do it. He won't make us trust and he won't make us believe and he won't make us obey. They require our own volition.

Unless we're confident that when we take our stand on God's word his sovereignty is upholding that word, we will stand tentatively and not for long.

Earlier we read that they that know their God will be strong and do exploits. The reverse is also true: they that do not know their God's integrity will be weak and do little. They will do only what they can accomplish on their own.

Unfortunately, when we believers—who carry the very life-giver within us—are called upon to go in Jesus' name to do his bidding, we'll go timidly, if at all, unless we're confident we are going with the force of his sovereign right and power to rule backing up his word.

Surely, in order to be all we are called to be in this world, we need to know we aren't alone. We need to be aware that God not only wants us to *trust* him, he also wants us to *believe* him. He wants us to expect that he will keep his word.

He knows we need that kind of confidence in him. That's why he let us know through the recorded words of the psalmist that he has exalted his word above his name—so we will put our faith in what he has said no matter how long ago he said it.

If what I've told you here is true, what implications does it have for your life? And what effect on your destiny if dealing successfully with earth's giants and mountains is part of the great and exciting works you were born to do?

As you search God's word and listen to your heart you will find the direction you need to scale the mountain that blocks your path. Or maybe you'll cast it aside as Jesus said in Mark 11:23, "Whosoever shall say to this mountain, Be thou removed, and be thou cast into the sea; and shall not doubt in his heart, but shall believe that those things which he saith shall come to pass; he shall have whatsoever he saith."

See that? Jesus said you have the ability to handle mountains.

But what about the giants you face? They are far more dangerous than the mountains. Your mountain will just sit there and even though it may keep you from moving forward or keep you from something that belongs to you, you can ignore it even while you pitch your tent in its shadow. Giants, however, are a different matter.

Just like David's Goliath, your giants are actively trying to steal, kill, and destroy. (John 10:10) What will you do about them? How will you slay the giant that threatens your life or inheritance?

You can do what David did.

The other day I watched a movie depiction of the life of David. In the scene with Goliath, they show David walking timidly toward the giant and finally stopping and staring, appearing to be somewhat mesmerized. Then, silently, he picks up a stone, puts it in his sling and lets it fly. He misses. After several tries, looking a little frazzled by now, David manages to hit Goliath in that one vulnerable spot on his forehead.

I was disgusted.

Typical of many Hollywood portrayals of Biblical events, they missed the whole point and left out the best part!

Yes, David used a little stone in his sling that day, but his real strength—that the Hollywood director didn't see or couldn't show us—was the confidence in God that was behind the words he boldly yelled at Goliath, "This day will the Lord deliver you into my hands!"

Isaiah 30:15, quoted under the title of this chapter, says that our strength is found in quietness and confidence. The confidence it refers to is our confidence in God. That confidence is our strength—not just to endure, but to do, to accomplish, and to take care of business.

So, then, take your cue from a young shepherd. First, find out what God has already said about your giant. Then do a little yelling of your own. As you do, you might just find at your feet some special stones designed perfectly for a giant's head.

That's the gospel in a nutshell, isn't it? Believe in your heart, confess with your mouth, and act on what you believe.

Romans 10: 9, 10 told us all about it: "If thou shalt confess with thy mouth the Lord Jesus, and shalt believe in thine heart that God hath raised him from the dead, thou shalt be saved. For with the heart man believes unto righteousness and with the mouth confession is made unto salvation."

Remember David's dark night in Ziklag?

David was "greatly distressed; for the people spoke of stoning him, because the soul of every man was grieved every man for his sons and for his daughters" and, as 1 Samuel 30:6 also tells us, he "encouraged himself in the Lord his God".

As Bill Johnson said, the Bible account doesn't tell us how David did that. We know he wept bitterly with the others. We know he was despairing of his life. We know, too, that he cried out to God and said, "What do I do now?"

If we look carefully, we'll see he also did just what we have been talking about. He readjusted his sight and put his eyes on God.

Maybe he thought of the vanquished bears, lions, and giants of years gone by. Maybe he simply recalled a day, long ago, at his father's house in Bethlehem when the prophet Samuel anointed him to be the next king.

It may have been in remembering God's promises and faithfulness that David found the courage to obey God's new directive and to believe the promise that accompanied it: "Go, and you will recover all."

David turned from his despair, effectively changed where his men were looking, encouraged them to pursue their enemy and, finally, led them to victory as they reclaimed their families and goods from the Amalekites.

As you read this, you may be experiencing troubles of your own. You may be scared and even despairing. If you are, don't be too hard on yourself. After all, we just saw a man after God's own heart—killer of bears, lions, giants, and ten thousands—in trouble and scared.

Just do what David did that day. Turn your eyes away from the mess around you and encourage yourself in the Lord your God.

That's what I did that cold night in February when the combination of chemotherapy and anti-nausea drugs kept me awake yet again. One more time, I took my eyes off what I was going through, off what history said could happen, off statistics and all other distractions, and got them once more on a faithful and loving God who, as it says in Psalm 103, "redeemeth thy life from destruction."

I encouraged myself in the Lord, and so can you.

Don't even look inward to see what you may identify as only mustard seed faith. All faith looks like mustard seed before it's planted and given time to bring that mustard plant into the light of day. Keep your eyes on God, on his integrity, on the perfect love he has for you and the word he has already given you. As you do, your fear of giants and mountains will give way to quietness and confidence. That's where your strength lies.

In God's word, he not only shows you who he is, he also shows you who you are—the "new creature" that he created you to be. Without that knowledge and the rest of the wisdom the Bible offers, you have nothing before your eyes but your giant, yourself, and whatever resources you can find around you.

But there is so much more to this world than what you can see around you! Faith, the force that comes from believing God's word, connects you with his strength—the source of power that will help you walk this valley called earth and walk it strong, with the courage to be all you were created to be.

There's an unforgettable and heartbreaking line spoken by Marlon Brando in the movie *On the Waterfront*. He says, "I coulda been a contender. I coulda been somebody."

I wonder if some of the tears God will wipe away when we get to Heaven will be there because we have finally realized, "I could have done what God wanted me to do. I could have been an overcomer. His grace was sufficient. He told me so, but I wasn't sure I could believe it."

Thinking about Chapter Seven

Self Discovery Questions:

1. Have you ever felt unworthy of God's favor?
2. Do you think it's unfair that faith might be the kingdom's currency?
3. What would be a better currency?
4. What is meant by the saying: Self-righteousness is as filthy rags?

Truth Chaser's Prayer:

Father God,

Your ways are higher than my ways! Your way is full of grace and mercy, and your wisdom planned the "by grace, through faith" principle. Help me to walk in your ways.

CHAPTER EIGHT

Guard Your Heart

"The devil can cite Scripture for his purpose."
WILLIAM SHAKESPEARE
The Merchant of Venice

8.

"Keep thy heart with all diligence for out of it are the issues of life."
~ Proverbs 4:23

In the first chapter, I suggested that somewhere along the way our perception of God's character has been distorted and we haven't even been aware that it happened. But it did happen, and it happened because we believed something that simply was not true.

Lenin once said, "A lie told often enough becomes truth." I'm sure he meant that a lie told often enough begins to sound so familiar we mistake it for truth, and it then becomes the accepted reality by which we live.

Where did the lies come from? I'm sure no one told them deliberately. Maybe we even thought them up ourselves; we're quite capable of doing that. We heard them, whatever their origin, and we believed them—strange ideas about God, ideas that he must be shocked at.

Well, perhaps he's not shocked but surely he must be disturbed.

There was a funny example of one such idea in an episode of the hit sitcom *Seinfeld*. George is talking to his therapist and says something to the effect that he's afraid to be too happy because God wouldn't like that.

I laughed at George, but I could understand his paranoia. I'm sure I probably thought the same thing at one time. I remember a saying that was common in my childhood and often used by parents when their kids were cutting up too much: "You'll be laughing on the other side of your face before the day is out." In other words, you may be laughing now but you'll be crying soon. Perhaps that was just another version of "God doesn't like it when you're happy."

Examples of that bit of misinformation abound. The other day, after my chiropractor had adjusted my out-of-place rib, he asked how I was feeling. I answered with an enthusiastic "Great!"

He quipped in return, "When the good Lord sees us with a grin on our face, he wipes it off. So just say you're doing better."

There it is again.

How on earth did the good doctor and George and I believe such a thing, when God's word tells us in Proverbs 17:22, "a merry heart does good like a medicine," and Psalm 16:11, "in thy presence [God's presence] there is fullness of joy and at thy right hand pleasures forever," and much more about the subject, all of which should convince us that God, like any father, loves to see his children happy?

I don't know how we came to believe it but we did. Because of it, George and I, as well as my chiropractor and probably countless others, walked for a while in a measure of darkness.

There are other lies. I'll bet you can think of some you've heard and perhaps believed. Just watch a little television and you'll hear more than a few. Of course, it's just TV, just entertainment, and in many cases just a joke, but if we spend too much time away from our own reading of the Bible, the lies we hear from the media and other sources appear true.

Why does that happen? I think it may be the same reason a field left alone, untended, will go to weed. Jesus told us his kingdom worked much like a farm. In the Bible, our hearts are often referred to as a garden, a place where God's word is sown to produce a harvest and a place we are to guard and tend, for out of it are "the issues of life".

The words we speak and the things we do, whether good or bad, all come, the Bible tells us, from our heart.

Earlier, I mentioned the eyes of our heart and the importance of what those eyes look at. It's in our heart that our future is formed—a future irreversibly connected to the picture of God that we see, or don't see, there.

The other day, a friend forwarded to me this story about a little girl in kindergarten, painstakingly drawing something. The teacher says, "Tell me about your picture." She knows that one should never ask a kindergarten child *what* it is they've drawn; one is expected to be able to recognize what it is.

"It's God," the little girl answers.

Her teacher tells her kindly that no one knows what God looks like.

"They will in a minute," she replies.

We're so like that little girl. We sometimes draw our own picture of God based on bits of information we have heard or based on what we have seen and experienced of the darkness of this earth and attributed to him. Unfortunately, our picture may not look at all like God.

In the information age we live in, knowledge abounds and is available at the click of a mouse. Misinformation also abounds and is just as available.

To clearly see God, we have to go where he has drawn his own picture.

From Genesis to Revelation, God carefully and patiently paints a picture of himself, telling the story of his loving pursuit of his children and inviting us to know him. Only there can we recognize who he really is.

As he takes us through the scriptures from the time and place where his light and glory were bright—the Garden of Eden— through millennia of darkness where his light was small, we arrive at the turning point of time, when Jesus came and showed us the Father as he walked among us.

One day as Jesus was walking he stopped by Jacob's well in a city called Sychar, in Samaria. He struck up a conversation with a Samaritan woman and, during their chat, he tells her, "You worship *you know not what*...but the hour comes and now is, when true worshipers will worship the Father in spirit and *in truth*: for the Father seeks for such to worship him."

Can you hear it in his words? God wants us to worship him with a true picture of him in our hearts.

In Truth

An embarrassing incident that occurred at my wedding reception many years ago illustrates painfully what I'm talking about. A popular wedding tradition in those days was to have someone give a toast to the parents of the bride. I had asked my parents' pastor to perform this duty for me. When he stood up to toast my parents, it was obvious that I had inadequately communicated my request, because he began a toast to me, of whom he knew very little.

At first I thought all would be well, since he was saying such lovely things. In fact, I was really quite enjoying what he had to say about me, and thought this wasn't going too badly after all, when my hopes were dashed.

The problem was that everyone who knew me soon realized what had happened when he talked about what a great cook I was. He had no doubt dined at my mother's table and assumed I had paid attention during my youth and learned from this expert. I had not. I was horrified to hear not-very-well-disguised snickers from a few of my nearest and dearest friends. The loudest snicker, more of a guffaw, came from one of my bridesmaids—my former apartment mate, Gloria, who had endured more than one of my burnt offerings.

Oh, how I hoped the pastor's praise for my culinary skills was prophetic, but time has proven that, alas, it was not. It was a toast without knowledge—praise without truth.

On The Day of the Glimmer mentioned in Chapter One, when my heart kept me from continuing what I have since called fake praise, I was doing something very similar to what that dear pastor did—only it was much worse. I was worshiping, or at least speaking words of worship, without understanding what I was saying. I was worshiping without truth. The words themselves were truth; they just weren't my truth.

Jesus words to the woman at the well in Samaria show that God wants our worship to spring, almost unbidden, from the truth about him we hold in our hearts. Only then is it true worship, the kind one of my favorite authors, Laurie Beth Jones, has written about. She says, "Worship puts us in touch with the divine, and when we are in touch with the divine we rise to our highest and our best." (85)

Scattered throughout the Bible there are many statements of what worship does for the worshiper. Not the least of these benefits is one that is obvious and, in fact, one that Laurie Beth Jones' statement speaks to: It helps us stay focused on our Father and helps us walk with him. Jesus said the Father is looking for such worshipers; he wants worshipers who know him. Let's not settle for less than he wants.

Not settling takes diligence. Whenever I notice that strange ideas, lies about God, are beginning to filter into my thought processes, I have a checkup psalm that I go to—a sort of heart monitor. Psalm 103 is not the only place in scripture that we clearly see God, but it is so easy to see his heart for his children there. It may be good for you to read that psalm again just to refresh the picture your heart sees.

Not settling also takes the courageous and committed heart of a truth chaser, because although truth may reach the mind by casual hearing, it doesn't settle into the heart and become functional and fruitful without personal engagement.

Do you remember our first step in this process—the one Proverbs showed us? "Receive my words. Put your heart in it. Listen. Ask. Seek. Search for truth." Even though we know the speaker here is a man talking to his son, we commonly accept that it is God's wisdom for us as well. Get actively involved, he tells us, as you would in a search for something of great value.

Search as you would for gold.

When God put Adam in the Garden of Eden, he told him there was gold there and it was good. In Proverbs, he tells us there's gold in his word and it's good. Be assured it will take effort to find it, but it's worth every effort it will take.

Thinking about Chapter Eight

SELF DISCOVERY QUESTIONS:

1. Have you ever been worried that God might have bad plans for you?
2. Why have you thought that?
3. Can you think of any other misinformation you have accepted about God?
4. Where did it come from and why do you think you believed it?

TRUTH CHASER'S PRAYER:

Dear Father,

Help me to recognize what is true and what is false. Please help me to find the gold. Help me to worship you in truth.

CHAPTER NINE

How Does Your Garden Grow?

"Nothing will come of nothing."

WILLIAM SHAKESPEARE
King Lear

9.

"Behold a sower went forth to sow."
~ Matthew 13:3

We crawl into bed exhausted and sleepy. As we reach to turn out the light we see the Bible sitting reproachfully on the night table. Luckily, we know how to get rid of the guilt that just jumped into bed with us. Psalm 134 or 150—one of the short ones—will do. Or maybe even a whole chapter of Proverbs, especially if we missed yesterday's reading.

I'll bet there are more than a few of us would-be followers of Jesus who recognize that scene.

There's definitely nothing wrong—in fact there's everything right—with wanting to have a daily Bible reading. But when did reading the Bible become one of our daily chores, something we have to do in order to feel as if we have accomplished all we need to do before putting head to pillow? When did it become just another demand for our time in an already crowded life?

It's not supposed to be that way. You know it; I know it; all God's children know it.

And God knows it.

In fact, even though scenarios and feelings like those I've just described are probably too familiar, I believe we have always known at some heart-level that the Bible was and is a gift to us—a marvelous, precious gift that is meant to benefit us.

The metaphors we have been looking at that describe his word—light, gold, bread, and seed—all show us that God wants our time spent in his word to be more than something we do to prove our devotion or to collect those infamous Brownie points. The images evoked by these metaphors show us that his word is necessary to our very existence as Christians.

Our ability to wholeheartedly respond to God's word in the way he wants us to is what this book is all about. This last chapter is a look at some of the ways the psalmists with whom we began our journey responded to God's word. They will bring it all together for us.

Psalm 106 shows us one more time that our first response to what God says is to *believe it*. In that psalm we find the root cause of the trouble the children of Israel found themselves in. They "believed not his word...and they hearkened not unto the voice of the Lord" (Psalm 106:24, 25).

They didn't believe God so they didn't do what he said.

As we read the Israelites' story, perfect hindsight makes it clear that not believing God will put us on an eventually destructive track. As we follow the Israelites through the wilderness we see that the opposite is also true. Believing God is a *prerequisite* of walking the right path.

I have occasionally wondered how the children of Israel could be so blind as to disbelieve God. Think of all they had seen him do! But maybe it's our own blindness that keeps us from recognizing the moment *we* start walking down the same wrong road as they.

"But," I hear you saying, "I wouldn't read the Bible if I didn't believe it."

I did.

I read it faithfully for years and didn't believe it.

I did intellectually affirm that it was true, and I certainly tried to live by the parts that told me things like: Don't steal; Don't lie; Don't forget the assembling together. I definitely *thought* I had that first response covered. If anyone had asked, I would have said I believed because I affirmed the veracity of the Bible.

However, I only accepted and put into practice—or at least tried to—the parts that gave me something I felt I could handle on my own. Unfortunately, that list of "do's" was quite limited.

Sadly, there was a lot said in my Bible that I believed intellectually but consistently left on the night table, on those pages between the leather covers.

In 1985, when I heard of my sister's heart-shattering diagnosis and prognosis, as mentioned in the dedication of this book, I prayed that dangerous prayer, "I'm going to read your word as if I've never seen it before, and I want you to speak to me through it." I found out that night just how much of that word I had never really believed.

In desperation, I opened my Bible at the gospels and for hours followed Jesus on his travels, open to what I might hear from him. I listened to his gentle voice as he told the people, "Fear not, for you are of more value than many sparrows." And, he said, God watchfully cared for the sparrows individually. I'd always had a difficult time accepting what that meant for me.

Then I heard him say, "Ask, and it shall be given you; seek and ye shall find; knock and the door shall be opened to you: For everyone that asketh receiveth; and he that seeketh findeth; and to him that knocketh it shall be opened," and I knew I had never wholeheartedly believed that in all of my then twenty years as his disciple.

When he told the desperate father of a tormented boy, "If thou canst believe, all things are possible to him that believeth," I had to face the fact that I had never taken those words seriously—at least, not enough to believe all things were possible to me, too, if I would believe him.

I even thought I might have caught him in a lie when I heard him say, "If ye abide in me and my words abide in you, ye shall ask what ye will, and it shall be done unto you."

Of course, I knew it must be true because he said it, but to me, somehow, it didn't seem possible he actually meant it. I couldn't imagine anyone on earth having that kind of relationship with our Creator.

As I sat and stared at the words on the page—"ye shall ask what ye will and it shall be done unto you"—it suddenly hit me that if there was no circumstance in which these words were true, then they were, actually, a lie.

I was stunned.

It slowly dawned on me that somewhere in time, space, and experience there had to be a circumstance in which these words were true.

What a place that would be to spend your days!

The words of the beginning phrase, "If you abide in me and my words abide in you," sent a shock through me when I realized they described that place.

At that moment, the truth chaser inside me—long buried by years of disappointment and intimidation, and long since replaced by polite apathy—was resurrected.

That was more than twenty-five years ago and since that night I've never doubted the integrity of God. I've faced giants and I've stared up at a few intimidating mountains. I've needed my hope renewed occasionally and my courage restored, and there have been too many times I've failed to listen and obey, but I've never doubted that God would hold fast to his words and I've never been sorry I prayed that prayer. It led me to treasures that have empowered my journey ever since.

I found out that reading God's word is just the beginning, the sowing of the seed. I discovered that the wise sower will follow through and care for the seed until it produces its fruit. The book of Joshua lets us know how to follow through. It shows us how to take the word with us through the day.

At the beginning of the book, Joshua has been given a job to do. He's taking over the leadership role vacated by Moses, and he's getting some "how to" advice from God—how to make his way prosperous and have good success in this new endeavor.

God says, "This book of the law shall not depart out of thy mouth; but thou shalt meditate therein day and night, that thou mayest observe to do according to all that is written therein" (Joshua 1:8).

In that one verse we see three ways we are to respond to God's word after hearing and believing it.

The first of these three is simple: We talk about what he said. We talk to him and we talk to ourselves. We keep what he said in our mouth, even when it doesn't appear to be true at the moment and even when what he said we should do looks like a bad move. A key to doing this is found in Psalm 119:128, "I esteem all thy precepts concerning all things to be right."

All his precepts concerning all things! That might be tough, but it's doable. It simply means we agree with God.

When revenge looks good, we esteem forgiveness to be right. When hate feels natural, we choose to love. When we feel lonely, we esteem God to be our constant companion. When despair looks appropriate, we esteem hope to be right. When destruction looks inevitable, we esteem him to be our deliverer from destruction. When doubt rushes in, we esteem faith to be the responsible choice—because he said so.

Obviously, his ways are higher than our ways; his thoughts, than our thoughts. They are so much higher they may seem unnatural to us, but the next step helps with that.

According to God's advice to Joshua, the next step is this: We mediate on what God said. The more we do so, the wiser his ways and his thoughts appear.

That might sound like a practice associated with Eastern religions but, actually, if Joshua had to do it, we do too. Not to worry, though. It's easy. We meditate all day long; we're experts. We meditate on problems at work, on challenging relationships, on health issues, on new furniture we would like to buy—on something. It's just natural.

But God is telling us that in all our meditating we must not just *consider* what he has said but also make it the bottom line in our mental manipulations. (He definitely has said something that can relate to those problems at work, or those health issues, or even difficult children. He might even have something to say that will affect when and how we buy that furniture!)

Psalm 119:24 is our next step and coincides with the third of God's instructions to Joshua. It says, "Thy testimonies also are my delight and my counselors."

A counselor gives insight and helps us initiate appropriate action. God's testimonies, precepts, laws and promises are meant to do that. When we esteem God's word to always be right in every situation we are pretty close to that step where we let it be our counselor. When we hear or read the stories of what God has said and done in the past, they become prophetic of what he will do in the future. As we read his precepts and laws, they become the wisdom that directs our own actions. When that happens, God's word has become light to our path. We have learned to "observe to do,"—Joshua's step three.

Finally, God meant for his word to bring us hope—an expectation of future good. In Psalm 119:52 the afflicted worshiper says, "I remembered thy judgments of old, and have comforted myself." The stories of God's just judgments, steadfast faithfulness, and promised blessing are able to comfort us and calm us in the middle of our storms.

In verse 49 of that same psalm, the psalmist is praying and although it seems he's trying to convince God to help him, he actually is letting God know he's hanging on to his word for dear life: "Remember thy word unto thy servant, upon which thou hast caused me to hope; this is my comfort in my affliction: for thy word has quickened me."

His word can only fulfill this purpose if we read it, believe it, meditate on it, talk about it, let it counsel us, and give it time to create hope in us. If his word is to give us hope, then we have to know his sovereignty upholds his word.

As we do this, as we carry God's word in our heart, it will not only change our actions, it will transform our expectations. It will create a new vision of what can be.

When we follow this path laid out by the psalmists we eventually find ourselves at a place described by verse 162 of this same Psalm, "I rejoice at thy word as one that findeth great spoil."

Great spoil! Isn't that what we've been talking about all along? At last, we recognize the treasure.

Reading our Bible is no longer a chore. We see God's word as the light that shows us where to walk. It becomes the necessary bread that daily gives us the strength to live. We begin to value its treasures as the silver and gold that bring beauty and empowerment to our walk on this earth, and we treat his word as precious because it is the God-given seed of our God-ordained future.

Can you imagine the future that will spring from that seed? Think of it: you, a successful workman that needs not to be ashamed, becoming all God created you to be, accomplishing all that he calls you to do, and living the abundant life Jesus said he came to give.

Is the thought slightly disturbing?

In the book of Matthew, Chapter 5, Jesus is sitting on a hilltop looking around at a small group of ordinary people—a couple of rough fishermen, a government worker, a couple of rowdy guys he called Sons of Thunder, and others—and beyond them, a multitude. He began to teach them some important things about light. He told them, "You are light."

They are? He can't be serious.

Yes, they are light.

Then he tells them, "Shine."

The fact that he had to tell them to shine indicates three things: shining doesn't happen automatically; they have a choice to make in regard to this light; and they could possibly choose wrongly.

Why would they make the wrong choice?

Maybe they're afraid.

Our own response to Jesus' words—excitement or discomfort—will tell us whether or not we're afraid of our light.

What happens in a dark world if those who *know* the light, *have* the light, and *are* light are afraid of their light? You know the answer to that: There is nothing to dispel the darkness.

None of us is an island. Our lives and destinies are inextricably intertwined. We have a responsibility to those who walk with us.

That's why we can't allow ourselves to be frightened by the light God gave us. We have to embrace it and share it.

But how do we get rid of the fear? And how do we shine? We start by taking the light off the night stand.

As we fully respond to God's word we fully respond to him, and as his word becomes all he intended it to be in our lives we'll know we were designed to go higher—that we were meant for more than mere survival, for arriving safely in Heaven, as precious as that hope is.

Even though eternal life in God's presence is our goal, his gift of "life more abundant" starts here. He has designed, purposed, and empowered us for good works and great exploits and for righteousness, peace and joy on our earth-walk in his presence and in his light.

All of these things—our right standing with God, our unreasonable joy and peace in times of turmoil, our good works and exploits in his name—come only from him; they are all his doing and his word is the seed from which they come.

It truly is God who calls us upward, and he calls us with words. Even the impressions we receive in our heart are translated to our conscious mind as words. We really do partake of God's divine nature, experiencing all that he is and receiving all that he lovingly provides, through his words—his precious promises.

No wonder the psalmist praised God for his loving kindness and truth when he thought of the priceless treasure of Psalm 138:2. The bright and beautiful truth that God has magnified his word above all his name is indeed fine gold.

On this time-encased planet everything has a beginning. Robert Richardson, in his book *Emerson: the Mind on Fire,* says that "on a day no different than the one now breaking" (555) extraordinary things have begun. He writes about a time when the works of Shakespeare, the beauty of the Mona Lisa, and the music of Beethoven simply didn't exist. But then on some ordinary day, perhaps sunny, perhaps rainy and grey, the journeys began which led to beauty that has graced generations.

It is doubtful those artists knew at the outset every line of poem or play, every stroke of brush, or every note that was yet to be. But that didn't stop them. Undaunted by the time their journeys would take, they began.

On this very day you can begin something extraordinary: a new way of life, characterized by trust in God and faith in his word.

It may be a small beginning, as beginnings usually are, but from this day forward you will never be counted with those "cold and timid souls" of whom Theodore Roosevelt spoke, who know neither victory nor defeat, but rather with the valiant for the faith, who climb mountains of obedience, refuse to be cowed by fiery furnaces of persecution, and run to giants, shouting the word of their God as they go.

Go ahead. Let the exploits begin.

Thinking about Chapter Nine

SELF DISCOVERY QUESTIONS:

1. Which of God's seeds are already sown in your heart?
2. What fruit do you see from those seeds?
3. Are you willing to search the scripture to find the many seeds God has provided for the good harvest that is your divinely intended future?

TRUTH CHASER'S PRAYER:

Dear Father,

How faithful and kind you are! Your loving kindness and truth are my daily comfort. Your every word is precious. Thank you for each of them, and thank you for Jesus, the Word made flesh who showed us your true glory when he lived among us and still does today. Thank you for your Holy Spirit, my Comforter, Teacher, and Guide. By your grace, through faith—with my eyes on you and listening intently to your voice—I'll finish with joy the course you've set before me.

APPENDIX ONE
When God Relents

In the story recorded in Exodus 32, where Moses withstood God, we saw that God relented and did not do what he said he wanted to do—that is, destroy the Israelites and, in their stead, make of Moses a great nation. I can imagine that some, reading this and other stories where God changes a declared plan, might think, "There! God doesn't always hold fast to what he says!"

In these stories, and perhaps in all stories of such kind—for example, that of Jonah and his preaching to the city of Nineveh—I expect we will find that God's first declared plan of action was in accordance with his previously established words and, therefore, a legitimate response to the actions of the men and women involved.

His subsequent relenting was in response to the repentance of the people or even the requests of his servants, and, always, his new plan was in accordance with his mercy and his well-known will to restore and do good to his people.

Another such story is that of Hezekiah, recorded in 2 Kings 20.

God's prophet told the ailing Hezekiah what the future held for him—he would succumb to his sickness and die that very night.

In this instance, as in the others, because of God's great mercy and in response to Hezekiah's prayer—which seems to be one he loves to hear: I'm hoping in your word—God intervened on his behalf and healed him, giving Hezekiah fifteen more years.

So it would appear that whenever Biblical accounts suggest God is not upholding his word, it is actually that he is upholding his promise to forgive, restore, and bless when his people—even if only one in the whole group, as in Moses' case!—respond to him in hope, trusting in his goodness and his faithfulness to his word.

Psalm 106 gives a clear picture of how the story goes: The children of Israel, time and time again, turned from God's wisdom, did not believe his word, complained in their tents, and did not heed the voice of the Lord. Justice required that they eat the fruit of their folly. And so they did.

But time and time again, when they cried out to God, this was his response:

Vs. 44-45: "Nevertheless, He regarded their affliction when He heard their cry; And for their sake He remembered His covenant, and relented according to the multitude of His mercies." (NKJVim)

APPENDIX TWO
Different Translations of Psalm 138:2

Psalm 138:2 has been translated differently in different versions of the Bible. In some versions it appears the translators, in their attempt to make the text more understandable to modern day readers, found it difficult to stay close to the original. While this happens rarely and is not always a problem, in some incidences where the original language doesn't easily translate into modern day usage, the paraphrase that results may be limited by the understanding of the writers/publishers or even by preconceptions based on a previously established theological bent. I believe, therefore, it would be helpful to look at the way this verse reads in several of these translations and compare each to the rendering of the text in the original language, Hebrew.

The Interlinear Hebrew-Aramaic-Old Testament; Volume III of the Interlinear Hebrew-Greek-English Bible: "Will I worship/ sing will I praise to you/ the gods before/ my with heart whole/ will I you thank/ your truth for, and your mercy for/ your name, give and to thanks/ your holy temple toward/ you answered me/ I call in the day/ your word/ your all above name/ have you magnified for."

The English arrangement of these words according to this same Bible: "I will thank you with my whole heart; I will sing praise to you before the gods; I will worship toward your holy temple; and give thanks to your name for your mercy and for your truth; *for you have magnified your word above all your name."*

New American Standard: "I will give thee thanks with all my heart; I will sing praises to thee before the gods. I will bow down toward thy holy temple, and give thanks to Thy name for Thy loving kindness and Thy truth; *for Thou hast magnified thy word according to all thy name."*

New International: "I will praise you, O Lord, with all my heart; before the gods I will sing your praise. I will bow down at your holy temple and will praise your name for your love and your faithfulness, *for you have exalted above all things your name and your word."*

Amplified: "I will confess and praise you O God, with my whole heart; before the gods will I sing praises to you. I will worship toward your holy temple, and praise you for your loving kindness and for your truth and faithfulness; *for you have exalted above all else your name and your word and you have exalted your word above all your name."*

In two of these translations, the *NIV* and the *Amplified*, the phrase is rendered, *"you have exalted above all things your name and your word'"* The *Amplified* goes on to include the phrase as it appears in the closest translation to the original, *"for you have exalted your word above all your name."*

Whatever we read in the Bible must in its essence reveal God to us, show us what he's done, or tell us his will for man. At the very least, any words that we read, even in the Bible, must communicate something to us that is understandable and usable. Before we decide what each of these translations is communicating, we should look at each in the context of the whole thought.

The whole thought of our verse is centered on the reason for the psalmist's praise and worship. Since the psalmist is praising God for his loving kindness—also translated mercy—and truth, we know that the magnification of "*the word and the name*" or "*the word above the name*"—whichever is being communicated—showed the writer these characteristics of God.

If it is "*the word and the name*" that are exalted above "*all things,*" we have to ask how the exaltation of these showed God's mercy and truth. It may show us his power and authority, but not his mercy and truth.

The rendering in the *NAS*, "*for Thou hast magnified thy word according to all thy name,*" can be subjected to the same scrutiny as was the *KJV* in the text of this book by inserting the elements of a name: "*For thou hast magnified thy word according to all thy identity, character, reputation and authority.*"

Again, it's difficult to see what is being communicated here and what it has to do with loving kindness and truth. Both of these fall short of communicating anything that gives us reason to praise God for his mercy and truth.

The most beautiful paraphrase of that verse that I have found and the one I believe is closest to the spirit of what it is actually saying is found in *The Living Bible*.

The Living Bible: "Lord, with all my heart I thank you. I will sing your praises before the armies of angels in Heaven. I face your temple as I worship, giving thanks to you for all your loving kindness and your faithfulness, *for your promises are backed by all the honor of your name.*"

There it is: God's integrity, which is, I believe, what the text truly is all about.

References

Cahill, Thomas. *How the Irish Saved Civilization* Doubleday, New York, 1995.

Green Jay P, Sr. (ed.) *The Interlinear Hebrew-Aramaic Old Testament,* Hendrickson Publishers, Peabody, Mass, 1961

Jones, Laurie Beth. *The Power of Positive Prophesy* Hyperion, New York, New York, 1999.

Lewis, C. S. *The Chronicles of Narnia; The Voyage of the Dawn Treader,* Harper Collins, New York, 1980.

Richardson, Robert. *Emerson: The Mind on Fire,* University of California Press, Berkley and Los Angeles, 1995

The Comparative Study Bible, Zondervan, Grand Rapids, Michigan, 1984.

The Living Bible, Tyndale House Publishers, Wheaton, Illinois, 1971.

The Holy Bible, New King James Version, Thomas Nelson Publishers, Nashville, 1982

John Montgomery, Revolutionary Fifer

By

Pat Duffy

ISBN: 978-1-4269-9728-0 (sc)
ISBN: 978-1-4269-9727-3 (hc)
ISBN: 978-1-4269-9729-7 (e)

Library of Congress Control Number: 2011917586

Trafford rev. 03/27/2012

 www.trafford.com

North America & international
toll-free: 1 888 232 4444 (USA & Canada)
phone: 250 383 6864 ♦ fax: 812 355 4082

CONTENTS

Dedicated to my daughters, Peggy, Mary, Eileen, Ann, and Theresa.

And a special dedication to Willa Lynch for her research and encouragement.

Chapter 1

The rain had stopped and the two brothers playing checkers on the front porch occasionally glanced up as the North Carolina rain dripped from the overhanging branches of the poplar tree in the front yard. The farm was always busy, but rain meant leisure time because they could not work in the fields in the rain. Molly and Blossom, the family milk cows, were in the barn. Molasses, one of their horses, was in the barnyard and the chickens were clucking as they came out of the henhouse and scratched the earth.

"Ha," said Alex, the oldest, "I finally beat you this time."

"You did. But I am still the champion," John replied smiling and affectionately punching his brother's shoulder.

Their father, sitting on his willow rocking chair said, "Let's have some music, John. You need to practice anyway."

"I will, just as soon as I help Alex put the checkers away." His father rocked back and forth in his rocking chair. The harness he had repaired lay beside his chair.

"Play *The Banks of the Dee* please John please." His mother's raised voice came from the house. "It's my favorite song."

"I know it is."

"It's summer and softly the breezes were blowing . . . ." They heard their mother's voice as the aroma of fresh-baked bread wafted from the house. "I'll be out in a minute; the bread is just coming out of the oven."

Suddenly, down the lane came their neighbor, Mr. Reed, riding his horse as hard as he could. He rode up to the porch and dismounted quickly, tying the horse's reins to the hitching post.

"Good morning, Reed," Alexander Montgomery said pleasantly.

"I came as quickly as I could. It's war! War has been declared against the British. No more taxation without representation! No unfair taxes on tobacco or tea!" He sat down on the porch step, pulled a cloth from his pocket and wiped his flushed face. The group on the porch fell silent. John laid his fife in his lap.

"God help us, but we can beat the Redcoats. They have been in this country long enough. It will be a hard fight, as we will be outnumbered. We can win." Alexander stood up, squared his shoulders, sighed deeply and continued, "Remember the Indian fighting we have done, Thomas?"

"Yes," Thomas Reed answered softly.

"Martha, Mr. Reed is here." Alexander Montgomery called to his wife.

"Coming." She walked out on the porch, her apron dusted with spots of flour. She brushed the brown hair away from her face. "Welcome, Mr. Reed. How are Amanda and the new baby?"

"She's fine and the baby is now sleeping all night, thanks be to God," he replied. "Good morning, young Alex and John and Master Michael," he said, greeting the Montgomery sons with a smile. Michael took his thumb out of his mouth.

"Good morning, Mr. Reed," the boys said in unison. Michael's thumb went back into his mouth.

Mr. Reed's expression changed to one of concern. "I rode over to tell you that the Continental Congress declared war back in April."

Martha Montgomery covered her face with her hands. "Oh dear, I wish we could settle our differences without a war."

"King George would rather go to war than stop all this taxation. George Washington was put in charge by the Congress. He is a good officer and has a lot of experience." Mr. Montgomery motioned to his wife to sit in the rocking chair. He moved to sit beside Reed on the step.

"Does he know much about fighting the British?" she asked, her voice filled with worry.

"Well, Martha, he is an honorable man and a patriot. He will do the best he can, as we all will," Mr. Reed said with hope.

"Amen to that," whispered Montgomery.

"We'll fight, too," the young brothers said with conviction.

"John, Alex, you are too young."

"But Mother, we know how to shoot a gun. Just ask the rabbits here about," bragged John, his blue eyes bright.

His mother smiled and ruffled his dark brown hair with her hand. "That's right. I need you boys here to shoot rabbits so we can have rabbit stew."

To his father Martha Montgomery said, "I am worried about this war. War means lives are lost. And you know we don't even have a big army. The Redcoats are well equipped with guns and cannons."

"But dear, that is what Washington will do. He is organizing an army and he will be a good General. He has had experience fighting Indians. We have all had experience fighting Indians," Alexander Montgomery said with a catch in his voice. He absently touched the jagged scar where a Shawnee war club had grazed his arm. "I remember those battles very well."

"Aye," agreed Mr. Reed.

John watched as his mother put her arm on his father's shoulder. "What will you do, Alexander?" She could not hide the worry in her voice.

"I don't know," her husband answered thoughtfully, "but we must defend our rights and we must win. We can't let the

British tax us any longer. And I am tired of seeing Redcoats everywhere."

"I am going to fight; I have already told Amanda," said Tom Reed.

"But you have a new baby," said a surprised Martha Montgomery.

"Yes, I have, but Amanda has given me her blessing. If we want to have a great republic we have to fight for it." Tom Reed's fist hit the porch.

"I'd like to fight, too," said young Alexander. "I am the oldest son in this family."

"Alexander, you are only fourteen!" his mother said in a loud voice.

"I would like to be a soldier, too," John replied.

"John," his mother said startled, "you are only twelve!"

"But I'm strong and I've almost reached my full growth. I'm almost six feet tall. I know how to shoot and I can march." He stood up and raised himself to his full height. "Let me fight those Redcoats, I can beat them."

"Oh, dear me." His mother, a worried expression on her face, leaned back into the willow chair and looked pleadingly at her husband.

"I—I—I—" he started to reply, but then he brushed his hand across his tanned face and turned away from his wife.

Tom Reed spoke. "I must get back to Amanda. But first I'm going to ride over to the Ross's and give them the news." He stood up and grabbed the reins of his horse.

"Let me get a fresh loaf of bread for you and Amanda. It has just come out of the oven." Martha walked to the door, opened it, and walked into the house.

"Thank you for riding over here with the news, Tom. I will have to talk to Martha tonight. I want to fight the British, but I will have to reason with her and persuade her. I know Mose, my farm hand, can handle the fields if I am away fighting." Alexander paused. "You know, I think we can whip the British and the war won't go on for very long. Besides, right is on our side."

"That is so, Alexander." With a soft slap to his horse's neck, Tom mounted.

Martha came out with a fresh loaf of warm bread wrapped in a kitchen cloth. "Here, take this to Amanda. She is very busy with a new baby and she need not bake today. And we will be over to see the new baby soon."

Tom Reed took the bread and said, "Thank you. Amanda and I appreciate your thoughtfulness." He pulled on the reins and turned his horse. Looking back he yelled, "To victory!"

The Montgomery family on the porch watched him ride down the country lane as his horse's feet threw clods of mud into the air.

"Father, I want to join up. I'm fourteen and old enough to fight." Alex begged, his blue eyes flashing. "Please! You know I can shoot anything with my musket. Remember, I shot the wild turkey last month."

"No, son, you are too young to go to war." His mother grabbed his hand and squeezed. "You must not go." She turned to her husband, "You must not let him go," she pleaded.

"Martha," he answered, his voice just above a whisper, "we may not have a choice. There are so many British troops, we are definitely outnumbered. We want to be rid of the Redcoats and I am certain every able-bodied man will fight. And our oldest son is able-bodied and is a good marksman."

She sank into the willow chair. "I can't lose the father of my children and my son to war." Martha covered her face with her apron. She dropped her apron in her lap and dots of flour remained on her cheeks. "I'm not a true patriot, am I?" she asked to no one in particular. "I know we must win and be rid of the British, but I now realize how hard it will be."

"I will be all right, Mother. I know how to take care of myself. Don't you worry." Alex took his mother's hand and held it. "I can shoot those Redcoats," he boasted.

Pulling his thumb out of his mouth, five-year-old Michael bragged, "Me too. I'll whip those Redcoats." His thumb went back into his mouth.

"Michael, you are a brave boy," his mother said as she scooped him onto her lap and gently pulled his thumb out of his mouth. Michael's grin was almost ear to ear as he looked at his mother.

"I am brave. I can fight the Redcoats and I can fight the Indians." He laughed when his mother gave him a big hug.

John sat quietly on the porch railing listening to his family. He wanted to be a soldier too, but he decided to say nothing. He knew his mother was upset; he would wait before he said anything about fighting. He knew he would need a good argument to become a soldier. He could play the fife, and fifers were very important in battles. Fifers were the soldiers who piped orders to the men. Fifers—and drummers, too—led the army into battle and he could do that. He would be patient and wait before he told his mother he wanted to go to war.

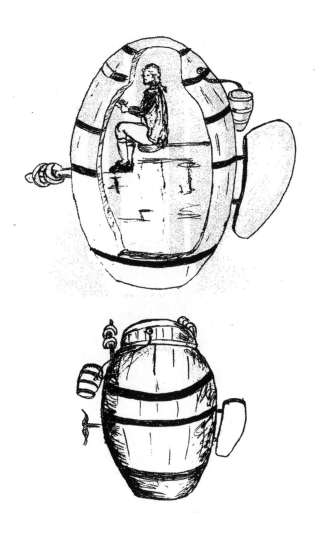

The Turtle Submarine

CHAPTER 2

The war continued, and the news was not always good. The British loyalists seemed to be winning. Then the colonists would defeat the Redcoats in a battle. News of the battles was received days or even weeks after each one happened. The colonists could not stop the British supply ships from bringing needed goods. John and Alex whispered about the events of the war each night when they went to bed. The brothers kept a list as they heard of the battles. On January 1, 1776, George Washington hoisted the first national flag in Cambridge, Massachusetts. This caused cheers from the Montgomery family and neighbors, but not from the Loyalists.

At the same time, Lord Dunmore's navel bombardment on Norfolk, Virginia, caused a terrible fire in the city. He occupied the city after both rebel and Tory homes were burned. But in February, the colonists recaptured the city. British General Howe abandoned Boston in February and the Continental Army occupied it in March. There was a naval battle in April, and the colonial ship, the *Lexington*, commanded by John Barry, captured a British warship. This action brought much celebration and cheers from John and Alex. Their joy was short-lived, as soon the British attacked Charleston, South Carolina, but Congress ordered General Charles Lee to Charleston to fight against the Redcoats.

The whole Montgomery family was excited when they heard that Thomas Jefferson wrote a draft of the Declaration of Independence. It was approved on July fourth and copies were sent to several state assemblies. "How I would like to see that document," their father said at the supper table one evening in late July after the news had reached them.

"I would like to read it myself," echoed their mother.

"Does that mean an end to the war?" asked John.

"No, not until we rid ourselves of the British," answered her father. "But Congress seems to be doing everything in its power to form our own country." He pushed back his chair and stood up. "Good supper, Martha. Let's have some music tonight, John, just before bedtime."

"Yes, Father." John said.

"The days are beginning to get shorter now and we must take advantage of the light." He stopped. "I'm going to check on the livestock. Boys, lock up the chickens; we don't need to lose any hens to the foxes. Ask Mose to help you get them in their henhouse." He walked outside and disappeared around the corner of the house.

Alex complained to John as they started for the chickens, "I'd rather be soldiering than chasing dumb chickens."

"So would I," answered John. He saw Mose, the field hand, and asked, "Can you help us round up these chickens?"

Mose smiled and replied, "Yes, sir." Mose quickly grabbed a clucking hen and put her in the henhouse.

The boys, smiling, chased several hens into the henhouse. There was much clucking from the hens and frustrated laughter from the boys. John actually fell down in the dirt. He got up smiling as he wiped the dust off his pants.

"Clumsy!" Alex shouted at him.

"Not as clumsy as you!" John retorted. After the chickens were in the coop the brothers went into the house.

When the evening's work was all done, the family gathered on the porch to listen to John's fife and to sing. Mose came and joined in with his deep baritone. Their first song was their mother's favorite, *The Banks of the Dee*.

'Twas summer, and softly the breezes were blowing,
And sweetly the nightingale sang from the tree.
At the foot of a hill, where the river was flowing,
I sat myself down on the banks of the Dee.

Flow on, lovely Dee, flow on thou sweet river,
Thy banks' purest stream shall be dear to me ever.
For there I first gain'd the affection and favor,
Of Jamie, the glory and pride of the Dee.

But now he's gone, from me, and left me thus mourning,
To quell the proud rebels, for valiant is he.
But, ah! There's no hope of his speedy returning,
To wander again on the banks of the Dee.

He is gone hapless youth, o'er the rude roaring billows,
The kindest, the sweetest, of all his brave fellows.
And left me to stray 'mongst these once loved willows,
The loneliest lass on the banks of the Dee.

"That's beautiful, Mother," praised Michael as he sat beside her. John and Alex nodded in approval.

"Let's do *The Liberty Song* next," said Alexander.

"It's a long one," said John. He wiped the mouth of his fife. "Ready?" He began to play and the family sang:

Come; join hand in hand, brave Americans all,
And rouse your bold hearts at fair Liberty's call.
No tyrannous acts shall suppress your just claim,
Or stain with dishonor America's name.

In freedom we're born, and in freedom we'll live;
Our purses are ready. Steady, friends, steady.
Not as slaves, but as free men our money we'll give.

Our worthy forefathers—let's give them a cheer,
To climates unknown did courageously steer.
Thro' oceans to deserts, for freedom they came,
And dying, bequeath'd us their freedom and fame.

Their generous bosoms all dangers despis'd,
So highly, so wisely, their birthrights they priz'd.
We'll keep what they gave, we will piously keep,
Nor frustrate their toils on the land or the deep.

The tree, their own hands had to Liberty rear'd,
They lived to behold growing strong and rever'd.
With transport they cried, "Now our wishes we gain,
For our children shall gather the fruits of our pain."

How sweet are the labors that freedom endure,
That they shall enjoy all the profit, secure.
No more such sweet labors Americans know,
If Britons shall reap what Americans sow.

Swarms of placemen and pensioners' soon will appear,
Like locusts deforming the charms of the year.
Souls vainly will rise, showers vainly descend,
If we are to drudge for what others shall spend.

Then join hand in hand brave Americans all,
By uniting we stand, by dividing we fall.
In so righteous a cause let us hope to succeed,
For Heaven approves of each generous deed.

All ages shall speak with amaze and applause,
Of the courage we'll show in support of our laws.
To die we can bear, but to serve we disdain,
For shame is to freemen more dreadful than pain.

This bumper I crown for our sovereign's health,
And this for Britannia's glory and wealth.
That wealth, and that glory immortal may be,
If she is but just and we are but free.

"How wonderful are the sentiments of this song," their mother said. "How good that John Dickinson wrote it."

There was thunder in the distance. "Looks like rain," their father said as the first drops of rain dotted the yard. "Off to bed, now." He turned to Mose and said, "Good night."

Mose echoed, "Good night," as he hurried out of the rain.

The family quickly changed into nightclothes. John and Alex climbed into bed, and Michael told his mother, "But I'm not tired," as he gave a big yawn.

Little did the Montgomery family know that they would awaken in the morning to news they could hardly believe.

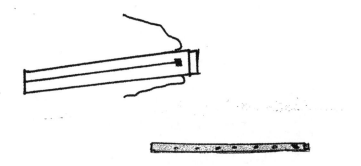

The fife and fife case: The fife was usually made of wood, especially boxwood; some were made of iron.

The snare drum was made of wood and painted light blue and tension was provided by ropes laced through holes.

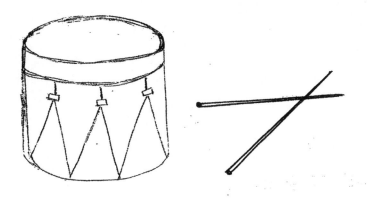

CHAPTER 3

"*A submarine? What* is that?" their mother asked in amazement.

"Well, as I understand it, it is a ship or boat that can go under water," Mr. Ross explained. "I brought this paper to show you, but it is quite unbelievable."

"It is. And to think we have a submarine and the British do not. They are better supplied than our forces are."

John, Alexander, and their mother and father sat around the table next to the hearth with Mr. Ross, discussing the information he had brought them. "The idea is to attach underwater explosives to British ships and blow them up." The family listened quietly as Mr. Ross continued to speak. "It is called the *Turtle* and was invented by David Bushnell of Connecticut, and Isaac Doolittle, a clockmaker, manufactured the firing mechanism."

"I don't see how it could go under water and not sink."

"Water was put in the bilge tank and hand-pumped out to rise to the surface. It was a one-man operation."

"And the owner didn't drown?" asked John.

"No."

"This is hard to believe," Mr. Montgomery stated, shaking his head in doubt.

"The sad thing is its function has failed, and the *Turtle's* transport ship has been sunk by the British. General Washington provided funds and had supported the development of the submarine," Mr. Ross continued. "An attempt to destroy HMS *Eagle* by Ezra Lee operating the *Turtle* failed in New York Harbor. The *Eagle* is Admiral Richard Howe's flagship."

"Sorry it didn't work," volunteered Alexander.

"Yes. What a good thing that would have been to destroy the British flagship," agreed his father.

Shaking her head, their mother asked, "Do you think a submarine is possible? A ship that can go under water and destroy other ships?"

"I think Bushnell has proved that it can be done, but I imagine it will take more experiments." He paused and sipped his coffee. "I suppose someday it will be possible for a man or men to go under water in a ship, but it is hard to imagine, isn't it?"

"We are in agreement on that."

"Would anyone like more coffee?" asked Martha. Her husband held up his cup, and she refilled it from the pot hanging on the hook. She shook her head when the boys looked eagerly at the pot and told them, "You boys have had enough." Resigned, John and Alexander set their cups back on the table.

"Thank you, Martha, for the coffee, but I must get home and tend to the plowing." Mr. Ross stood after drinking the last of his coffee and walked to the door.

"Thank you for bringing this interesting information to us. It is hard to comprehend such a thing."

Smiling, Mr. Ross said "Good-bye" as he put on his black hat, walked down the porch steps, and mounted his horse. He rode down the lane and was quickly out of sight.

"What do you really think, Martha, about the submarine?"

"I can't believe it."

"Neither can I. Now, boys, we need to go to the north forty and get started so we can plant some sweet potatoes." Father put on his hat as the boys got up from the table.

"Yes, father," the boys said. John and Alex pushed their chairs to the table and put their coffee cups on the dry sink. They were wearing their work overalls and shirts and dusty boots.

"We can finish before the day is over if we get to work," their Father encouraged.

Michael, who had sat quietly in the kitchen, said, "I want to come too. I am big, I can help."

His father smiled as he picked up his young son, "You can help. You get your hat and come with us. You have enough freckles on your face so be sure and wear that hat." He walked out the door carrying Michael on his shoulders with John and Alexander following.

Their mother rushed out the door behind them. "Here's Michael's hat," she said as she reached up and placed it on his head. "Now, help your father," she ordered Michael. He laughed as his father carried him to the field.

Tumpline

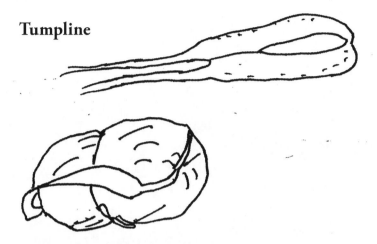

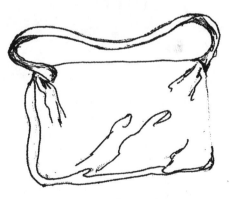

Tumpline rolled up. The tumpline was a strap placed around the chest and secured the soldier's pack of blanket, clothing and small items.

Haversack or knapsack for carrying soldier's personal equipment for his individual needs.

CHAPTER 4

In 1777, the southerners were greatly troubled by the war news. The British seemed to be winning many battles. John and Alexander over heard their parents talking after they had gone to bed.

"Martha, I do believe I will have to fight; I am going to volunteer. There will be major battles fought in the South. Cornwallis will be marching with his troops and coming this way."

"Oh, Alexander, I don't want you to fight. You have done enough fighting with the Indians."

"Martha, I have no choice. I'm going to see about joining up tomorrow. I will talk to Captain Snoddy. You know Mose can handle the farm if I am fighting."

"I don't want you to fight, but may God protect you, Alexander."

He leaned over, kissed his wife and settled down to go to sleep. Martha tossed and turned with worry and it was almost midnight before she closed her eyes and slept. Her sons, after hearing their parent's conversation, became excited and talked late into the night about joining up with their father. It would take some persuasion, but they knew their father would eventually give them permission. Their mother would not want them to go to war, and they worried about how to tell her. The last thing John whispered to his brother before they fell asleep was, "Somehow she will have to understand."

The next morning their mother remarked, "You two seem very quiet today. Are you feeling all right?"

"Yes, we're fine. John crowded me in bed last night."

"You took all the covers."

"Now, boys, don't start. If you are finished with your breakfast, help me hitch them to the wagon."

"Coming," said John. The boys rushed out the door with their father. As they walked to the barn John asked, "Where are you going?"

Their father paused, looked back at the house, and began, "I'm going to go see Captain Snoddy."

"Are you going to fight the Redcoats?" asked Alexander.

"I am. I've fought the Indians so that makes me experienced. I guess the rebels will need experience."

"Father, we want to fight, too," John pleaded.

"Yes, John and I do want to fight the Redcoats."

"Your mother will not want you to fight."

"But everyone knows that the colonists need soldiers. I am fifteen and I can shoot as good as you can." Alex stated emphatically.

"And I am thirteen and almost as big as Alex. I can shoot too. You know the colonists will need fifers," John said.

"I agree there will be a need for fifers, but you are so young. Your mother will skin me alive if I let you sign up."

"But Father, if Alex gets to become a soldier, I want to too," pleaded John.

Their father handed them the harness for the horses and the boys hooked them up to the wagon. Their father climbed up on the wagon seat.

"Please, let us go with you."

Their father looked up at the sky, paused, and moved his lips in silent prayer. "All right, I'm not saying you can become soldiers, but you can go with me."

John and Alex climbed up beside their father. They smiled at each other and knew that their father would let them become soldiers. Their mother, standing on the front porch with a worried look on her face, watched them go down the lane. She knew all three were going to join the fight. She could not blame them; the cause was just. She had to let them go. The three rode in silence for over a mile. They rode by the Russell homestead. There was a great deal of activity. Mr. and Mrs. Russell were loading trunks onto a wagon.

Their father said, *"Whoa,"* and the horses stopped. "I wonder what is going on here." He jumped down from the wagon with John and Alexander following him.

"Mr. Russell," they heard their father say, "It looks like you are moving."

Mr. Russell put down a chair he was carrying. "We are. We are going back to England."

"Going back to England?" asked a surprised Montgomery.

"I do not want to fight my neighbors, but my sympathy lies with the British. I am a Loyalist. I do not want to break with the crown." Mr. Russell looked at the three Montgomerys. "We are returning to England, and I don't know if we will ever come back to North Carolina."

"Mr. Russell, I am sorry to hear you are leaving. You have been good people and neighbors. I will miss you. Our whole family will. What will you do in England?"

"I have been offered a job in Kent. My brother lives there and he has helped me."

John looked around for Sara. "Where is Sara?" he asked Mr. Russell.

Alex poked John, "You are sweet on her."

"And what if I am?" He turned to Mr. Russell and asked again.

"Sara is in the house packing dishes. We hope to be aboard ship tomorrow and sail in two days."

John rushed up the steps. He entered the house calling, "Sara."

"In here," he heard her reply.

John walked into the room. Sara was busy putting dishes into a crate. "Sara," he said.

"Oh, hello, John." He saw the sad expression on her face.

"Sara, I'm sorry you are going to England." John's face showed the sorrow that he felt.

"I am sorry too. I don't care about the king. We are giving up everything and going back to England. I don't want my father to do this, but I have to go with the family." John saw tears well up in her eyes.

"I will miss you, Sara, and your brothers and sisters too."

"We will miss you too, John." She held a bowl in her hand. "My father does not want to fight with his friends and neighbors so we are going back to England. That silly king, what does he know about people living here?"

John smiled in spite of his sadness. He looked at Sara. He saw a beautiful girl with blond hair and blue eyes whom he liked very much. Suddenly he heard his father call, "John, time to be on our way."

"Sara, I have to go. My father, Alex, and I are going to become soldiers and fight the British."

"Good for you," she replied.

John thought for a moment. "I really will miss you, Sara. Would it be all right if I kissed you, a kiss for good luck?" He waited anxiously for her reply.

She leaned over and smiled and said, "I would like that."

John moved closer to her and kissed her on the cheek. "Remember me, Sara." He turned and hurried back to his brother and father. He was smiling broadly as he jumped back into the wagon. His brother and father smiled at him and he blushed. Then he turned pale; he had forgotten to ask Sara if she would ever return to North Carolina.

Iron camp kettles were used for cooking peas, beans, stews, soups and boiling meats.

Horn drinking cup was made of cow horn with a wood plug in one end. The soldiers were issued pocket knives and spoons for eating. The soldiers also had canteens made of wood, tin or sometimes glass.

CHAPTER 5

John and Alexander waited anxiously at Moore's Fort for orders. There were troops being sent out to quell Indian troubles, but John wanted to do battle with the Redcoats. The Indians were troublesome, continuing to attack settlers, and the soldiers spent most of their time protecting the frontier.

John practiced his fife every day with James the drummer. He knew every order from "go for water" to "go for wood." They marched until their feet were sore, but they became proficient in their duties. He was always ready for duty and was called upon many times a day to pipe an order. One day he was standing with the officers and others. He listened quietly as they talked about defending the settlers, the frontier, and the fort.

"Where are the Indians getting their guns? Did they steal from our stores?" Alexander Montgomery asked.

"No, as you know, the men take turns guarding our stores and supplies. There is no way they could get our guns and ammunition," replied Captain John Snoddy. "All of our weapons are accounted for."

Captain Reed said thoughtfully, "It has to be the British; they must be supplying the Chickamauga. Dragging Canoe, their chief, must be getting help from the Redcoats. Most of the Cherokee Indians are neutral."

"It has to be the British," Michael Porter said. "There are almost two hundred people here. Of course, the British would want to take this large fort here on the frontier."

"Let's be very diligent. I know you Scotch-Irish are the best fighters. And even if the British are paying the Indians for our scalps, we aren't going to let them have 'em. Keep all of your hair on your head!" Captain Snoddy's remarks made the men smile. "Montgomery, have your boy and the drummer sound 'go for water.' We better get a good supply of water from the Clinch River. One way the Indians could beat us is to keep us from having water. Our ladies want to wash some clothes and some muddy children. But I have told them to use the water sparingly. Each family will have just enough water for one tubful. Our new well is being dug."

John stepped forward when he heard his name.

"There you are, fifer." The Captain ordered, "Get the drummer."

"Yes, sir," John answered, and went to find James.

After the "go for water" had been sounded and the fort gates were opened, the wagons left with many empty barrels, wash tubs, large pots, and anything that would hold water. The wagons were escorted by men with rifles.

John sighed as the wooden gate closed. "There seems a lot to do that isn't actually fighting." He looked wistfully at his father. "Sometimes it can be dull around here."

With a forced smile his father told him, "John, men can be wounded or even die in battle. We can't be fighting every minute. Be grateful for free time, time away from fighting. Would you like to be a soldier on a long march in the heat of the day?"

John shook his head, "No, but I want to be a brave soldier."

"You are brave," his father said proudly, "and so is your brother, and James too. Soldiers sometimes have to be patient and always alert." John looked up at him and smiled.

"Think of our victory at Kings Mountain in South Carolina; that is still fresh in the minds of the soldiers. The Overmountain Men fought bravely. These men would not sign their allegiance to the king. They want their own country just like the colonists in the north. That October battle in '80 led by Colonel Selby and Colonel Campbell caused Lord Cornwallis to abandon his plans for invading North Carolina. Remember how the frontiersmen celebrated? The victorious yells of the men who won the battle I will remember forever. We captured 1,100 British forces that day."

John nodded. He thought he would never forget the noise of cannon fire and the shots and smoke of the guns.

"That victory and the recent victory at Cowpens have given the colonists much-needed hope. There is hope that we can beat the British, and there is hope that the war will soon be over," his father said. With his arm around John's shoulder they walked back together to join the others. The last thing his father said before they went inside the building was, "There will be plenty of fighting. I think we are going to move to have a chance to fight Cornwallis."

John said, as the heavy door closed behind him, "And that means plenty of marching."

"The Indians are wily and know the lay of the land better than anyone. They can hide in the woods and you never know they are there. They signal to each other with animal calls. We are here to get rid of the British Redcoats. I wish the Indians would help us, but they won't, so we must learn to fight like they do. Someday when the war is over we will get to go home and live in our house again."

"That is what I want, too." John brushed his brown hair away from his face and remembered their home with the front porch and the fields green with crops. But most of all he remembered his mother cooking, her hands covered in flower, making bread. He had wanted to join the fight for independence; he had not realized how hard it would be. He missed his home and all the good things he knew were waiting for him.

John's daydreaming came to an end when Sergeant Porter walked briskly up to him and said, "We are going to Whitsell's Mills to wait for Cornwallis. You and the drummer are needed in General Greene's office."

"Yes, sir," was John's reply as he went to find James.

John and James ready to do their duty.

CHAPTER 6

John looked in the doorway of Whitsell's Mills and saw Colonel William Washington, General Pickens, Colonel Preston, and calvary officer General Lee all huddled over a map. The officers were so engrossed in their work that they did not notice him. John heard General Greene say, "Cornwallis was camped at Clapps Mill on Alamane Creek, but he is marching with his men and will soon be here. He has many men, but I know our men will fight gallantly. Colonel Williams is evading the British and will be here, hopefully, before the Redcoats."

John walked away and found his father cleaning his musket. His brother Alex was helping. He had a rag and was polishing the rifle barrel. His father's powder horn was beside him. John told them, "The British will be here soon; I overheard General Greene." He turned and looked at General Greene from across the room. The general was a tall, imposing figure. The men respected him because he had had a lot of experience fighting under General George

Washington. General Washington had sent him to manage the Southern Campaign of the war.

"The British have us out numbered, but they forget that we have had practice fighting Indians and we can disappear into the woods. Trees are a good cover for fighting men," the Montgomerys heard the general continue.

Alex laughed, "It's hard to hide when you are wearing a bright red coat."

"Ha, the British think the back woodsmen are poor soldiers, but we will prove that we are fighting men." The boys' father stood up and suggested, "Let's go get some coffee before the battle starts." He picked up his rifle, and Alex and John followed him to the campsite.

The coffee pot was hanging on a hook over the red embers of a dying fire. Alexander Montgomery got horn cups and handed them to his sons. He poured coffee. "It will be hot, so be careful."

John didn't like coffee without sugar but he drank it anyway sipping slowly and trying hard not to show his dislike. After all, he told himself, soldiers can eat or drink anything. John would have preferred tea, but since the Boston Tea Party of 1773, the colonists drank mostly coffee.

The boys relaxed with their father and soon were smiling and laughing as they heard of Father's last trip home. Their mother was fine, and Mose was taking care of the fields. "Young Michael plays soldier and pretends the rabbits are the enemy. He is out every day shooting them with his wooden toy gun. He is also riding Molasses quite well. He always asks about you boys. And, of course, your mother is anxious for the war to be over so you boys can come home."

Alex said, "I can't wait to get home."

"Me too," John told them.

The sergeant hurried up to them. "Fifer, you are needed at headquarters."

"Is the battle about to begin?" questioned their father.

The sergeant nodded. "On the double, fifer."

John stood up and hugged his father. "Stay safe, Father," he whispered. To his brother he gave a salute and said, "Get those Redcoats, but don't let them get you." He turned and ran toward headquarters. He would soon be piping orders to the soldiers.

Soon the battle began. The fighting was intense. All you could hear were gun fire and shouting. Suddenly something strange happened. Colonel Preston's horse took a fright and headed for the British line. John knew it was Colonel Preston because he was such a big man. The colonel's horse threw him, then started to gallop back to the American line. The colonel couldn't keep up. Major Cloyd dismounted and gave his horse to the colonel. Colonel Preston rode back to the American line, and Major Cloyd ran behind him. John thought Major Cloyd was a true patriot. Colonel Preston would have been killed or captured if he had not been helped by the major.

Even with Colonel Williams arriving at the battle and engaging in a rear action fight, he was driven back. John and James had to sound retreat, and the Americans were ordered back to Guildford Courthouse. The injured were put in wagons, but many of them walked. John worried about his father and brother. He marched at the front of the retreating army and did not know until later that his father and brother were safe. As he watched the battle he had prayed silently that they were not hurt. How happy he was when he saw both of them with dirt on their faces and dust on their clothes, but not injured in any way. John had been afraid during the battle, not for himself but for his father and brother. It was then that John decided he did not like war.

Powder Horn

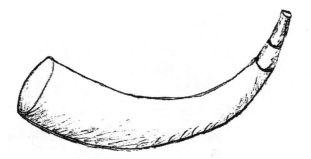

Chapter 7

It was days later that the soldiers reached Guilford Courthouse. John stood by his father and listened as General Greene gave the orders for his battle plan. Spies had told him the English General Cornwallis was coming with four thousand men. "It will be a hard battle to win, but the Redcoats will be fighting on our terms," General Greene said to his officers. "Our plan is this. There will be three lines spread over a half mile." He pointed to his map. "The first line will be one thousand North Carolina militia. Because our rifles can fire a longer distance these men only have to volley twice and then get out of the way. The British have bayonets and we will fight hand-to-hand." General Green looked at John's father who nodded that he understood. "On the right will be Lynch with two hundred Virginia riflemen, supported by Colonel William Washington with ninety dragoons, and Captain Kirkwood with the eighty man company of the Delaware line. On the left, Colonel Campbell will have two hundred Virginia riflemen, and Lee's legion of seventy-five horses and eighty-two foot soldiers. Also, fourteen hundred

Continentals from Virginia, Maryland, and Delaware with the Virginia Militia." Greene paused, waited for questions, and then began again, "We are outnumbered, but we have a great cause."

Just then a scout rushed into the room announcing, "Cornwallis is about a mile away."

General Greene pulled out his pocket watch. "Hmm, they will be here at about one thirty. Get your men in position. Fifers and drummers get ready for 'charge.' Good luck, men." The officers filed out of the room as well as the fifers and drummers. John felt the excitement in the air. He suddenly realized that he was not afraid. He would do his duty. Standing beside James, he picked up his fife as James picked up his drumsticks. Both boys smiled at each other and they gave the call to arms. Soon the soldiers were in place and impatiently waiting to hear the footsteps of the marching British soldiers.

The British, their bayonets ready, came out of the woods. The North Carolina militia shots rang out, and some British soldiers fell. The militia reloaded and fired again. Following orders, they ran away from the British with their shining bayonets. Cannonballs flew overhead. Many of Cornwallis's soldiers fell to the ground, wounded or dead. General Cornwallis ordered grapeshot fired at the Americans. His horse was shot out from under him, but a British soldier quickly rescued him. The Americans fought bravely as did the British. In the end the British were victorious, but they suffered so many losses that General Cornwallis's army was down to fourteen hundred men.

John played his fife as ordered by his commander. He watched the battle and was saddened by the loss of many men on both sides. James also played his drum as ordered. Both boys wished they had rifles to fight the British, but their commander said they had an important part in the battle keeping the soldiers informed of their orders.

John, short of breath said, "I don't think I can play another note."

"Yes, you can," answered James. He twirled his drumsticks in the air and gave John an encouraging smile. John wiped the end of his fife on his shirt and put the fife in his mouth as the battle raged around them. John secretly wished that the war would be over, but he and his brother had signed up for five years. He hoped his father and brother were safe. He couldn't see them as there was so much smoke from the guns it was difficult to tell who was who in hand-to-hand combat. He could distinguish the British with their red coats and he often thought that if they had worn anything but red they would be better disguised. It was hard to hide red in the woods or out in the open fields.

When the battle was over John went searching for his father and brother. He ran to his father when he found him at the edge of the battle field. He was on Molasses. John gave the horse an affectionate pat on the nose. Molasses nuzzled John's arm. His father's face was dirty and his clothes were too. He asked anxiously, "Are you all right? Please be all right."

"Son, I am tired but fine. There is not a scratch on me."

Alexander's strong arms hugged John and tears welled up in his eyes. Composing himself, John asked, "Is Alex safe? Is he hurt? Where is he? Have you seen him?"

"John, so many questions. Alex will be fine. The doctor is with him."

"Is he hurt? Tell me, Father, please," begged John.

"John, he is with the doctor. He has a small wound on his shoulder. Go to him, he will be glad to see you."

John turned and ran. He entered the makeshift hospital. Wounded soldiers were everywhere. The busy doctor was tending to a soldier with a wound to his eye. A large white bandage covered most of the soldier's face. He saw Sergeant Porter with a bandaged leg. John rushed up to him asking, "Sergeant Porter, are you hurt badly?"

"No, son, but I will be laid up for a few days."

"Can I get you anything or help you?" Sergeant Porter was one of John's favorite soldiers.

"I would like a drink of water."

"I'll get it." John rushed over to a bucket of water and carried it over to Sergeant Porter. He took the dipper and gave the sergeant a drink.

"Thank you, son." The sergeant lay back down on the floor.

Just then John saw his brother. He was sitting on a chair with a bandage on his shoulder. "Alex, are you all right?" He stood anxiously at his brother's side.

"Yes, John, I will be just fine in a few days. The doctor put comfrey leaves on my wound and then a bandage. He told me to keep it clean. I didn't get out of the way of a British bayonet. The doctor says that in a few days I will be all healed and ready to fight again."

"Alex, you're fighting with all your might. I am proud of you, but what will Mother say when she hears that you are wounded?"

Alex laughed, "We won't tell her, no need for her to worry. Besides it's just a small wound." He frowned when he moved his right arm. "It's a good thing I am left-handed, isn't it?" Alex laughed and put his left hand on John. John stopped worrying about his brother, leaned back against the chair, and sighing with relief simply answered, "Yes."

Just then their father walked up. His face was grim, but when he saw the two boys together he smiled broadly. "Are you doing all right, Alex?" he asked.

"I'm fine; doesn't even hurt very much." Alex replied.

"You are both very brave, and I am very proud of both of you."

The brothers smiled at each other and gave their father a big hug.

"Although we lost the battle, Cornwallis has lost a lot of men and many are wounded. It is a victory in name only. General Greene says the British cannot continue fighting when so many soldiers are lost. This war will soon be over. We are going back to Moore's Fort and I am going home. Soon your five years will be up and we will expect you at home. I know your mother will want to have a celebration when you come home. What a happy day that will be!"

"It has been a long time since we have been home," said John wistfully.

"It will be great to see mother and have some of her fresh bread and all the good things she cooks." Alex absentmindedly patted his stomach.

"You are always thinking of food," teased John. "But I would love a piece of apple pie or Mother's bread pudding."

"She will make both for you when you come home. In the meantime, take care of yourselves and keep safe."

They walked their father to the door and watched as he threw his leg over Molasses and joined a group of men. The boys stood in the doorway and watched until the men were dots on the horizon.

Lieutenant Oliver rushed in and announced, "We are retreating to Moore's Fort. The wounded are to be put in the wagons and the rest of us will march. We leave as quickly as possible. All able bodied men are to help with the wounded." He looked at Alex. "Are you able to walk?"

Alex answered, "Yes, sir."

"I will help him if he needs it, sir," John told the lieutenant.

"Good man, soldier," was the lieutenant's reply. "On the double, now! Fifer, get ready. We must march as soon as possible." And for emphasis he added, "We must reach Moore's Fort as soon as possible; we are retreating. Even though Cornwallis has won, he is weakened by the loss of so many men. The supply wagons will follow us. We must be quick!"

Drummers Call

Beat by duty drummer (& fifer) to assemble drummers (& fifers) just prior to the Reveilly.

Fife

Drum

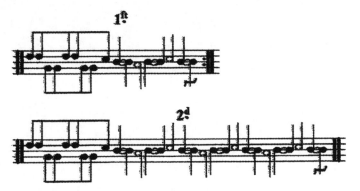

The first Part of the Drummers Call twice over, the second but once.

Chapter 8

The soldiers were on their way back to Moore's Fort. The regiment was camping along the river in tents. There were five men to a tent. John shared his tent with men he knew—Sam Walker, Joseph and James Miller, and Robert Green. The men had time to clean their muskets after setting up camp. They had cooked their meal of stewed turkey, corn cakes, and apples that Mose had brought to John. His mother had also sent him a letter, which raised his spirits because she knew how brave he was. Her letter was safely folded in his pocket. John knew he would read it again and again. It was James's turn to wash their cooking pots and their metal plates. John walked to the creek with James and sat on the ground by the water's edge. The water looked clear as it rushed downstream.

"You could give me a helping hand, John," James said as he dipped the plates one by one into the water, then into a bucket of soapy water.

"All right," John answered. "But you know it is not my turn to wash the dishes." He took each plate and dried them with a cloth. He put his hand in the cool water and then threw water on James. He laughed as the sprinkles of water hit James in the face.

"Aw," shouted James, turning and flicking water back at him.

John turned his head and the water thrown by James splashed on the back of John's head. John laughed and plunged his hand back into the water and threw some water back at James. The young boys were so busy splashing each other they did not hear approaching footsteps.

Suddenly lieutenant Oliver appeared from nowhere and barked, "Attention!" The two boys stood at attention, their hands dripping with water. Their smiles were erased from their faces, and the lieutenant ordered, "Back to camp."

"Yes, sir!"

The lieutenant turned and walked toward camp. John and James could not see the smile that crossed his face as he hurried away. The boys gathered up the washed tin dishes and horn cups and although subdued, they smiled quickly behind the lieutenant's back and walked back to their camp site.

The evening air was cool on their shirts, wet from the creek water. The roaring fire in front of their tent was a welcome sight. James and John gave a plate and cup and spoon to each of their tent mates. They sat down on a log by the fire. John brushed water from his dark brown hair and sighed. James tried to brush water from his shirt. "It will dry," volunteered John. He tried to hide a smile.

"I know," James told him. He grabbed an apple from the basket and began eating. The apple juice ran down his chin and he brushed it away with his hand. "Good apples, do you want one?"

"No, not now. You know my grandpa planted our apple trees. He loved apples. And my family has been eating apples from those trees for years; ever since I can remember. My grandpa was born in Ireland in County Down. I think it was in 1705. He came to the colonies and first lived in Pennsylvania. Grandpa married my grandma in Virginia and later moved to Rattlesnake Creek here in North Carolina. He was a believer in freedom, and he was a successful farmer. I know he would love to be here now." John stood and brushed corn cake crumbs from his uniform. "He would love to fight against all the taxation. I feel like he is here with me now, at least in spirit, telling me to keep on goin' and keep on soldiering."

"You know my grandpa had to fight the Shawnee when he came here. I guess it was bad, all that Indian fighting," James Miller said. James threw his apple core into the fire. He pulled out his tobacco pouch, took a pinch of tobacco and tamped the tobacco into his pipe with his fingers. He picked up a stick, held it over the fire and lit the pipe with it. He puffed on his pipe until there was a red glow. Smoke began to curl upward. "I'd like to be home, but I'm for the colonists' rights and against the king."

"I'd like to be home too, but this is our chance to fight against the Redcoats." John took a drink of water from his wooden flask and sat back down on the log. He stretched his legs out to the fire. "My parents work hard and giving their money to pay taxes is not fair. Grandpa would say, 'Now John, take care of the wee one and help your mother.' He would tell my older brother Alexander to take care of me. And if he were here today he would tell my brother and me to be the best soldiers we can be. You know, he is the one who encouraged me to play the fife."

"It's a good thing he did because you get to be a soldier and help in this war with the Redcoats," James told him.

"Yes, and I get to serve with my father and brother. Seems there is a lot of fighting here in North Carolina; first the Indians and now the British. I hope we will be through with fighting someday soon. My grandpa always said fight to win.

That was his motto, whether he was fighting Indians or bad weather when he farmed."

"That's a good motto." James continued to puff on his pipe. "My grandpa fought the Indians, too. And in '73 both of our fathers fought in Dunmore's War with the Indians. Daniel Boone's son was killed, remember? And so was William Russell's son. That fight went on until just about four years ago." James puffed again and the smoke blew around them.

"That pipe sure does smell good." John sniffed the air.

James took his pipe out of his mouth. "Want a puff?"

"Oh, I have never smoked in my life." John shook his head.

"Go ahead and try it. It's comforting to smoke a pipe." James held his pipe near John's face so he could smell the sweet tobacco.

"Ah we-e-l-l, I don't know," hesitated John.

"Just take a few puffs. If you don't like smoking you don't have to smoke. No harm in it. And you might like it," encouraged James.

John grabbed the pipe from James. "It does smell mighty nice and as you say, no harm in trying." John took a long puff on James's pipe. He coughed and nearly dropped the pipe.

"That's to be expected. Since you aren't used to smoking, you might cough a little. I forgot to tell you about that."

John coughed again and again. "I don't know about this."

"You need to wait a minute. Just take it slow and easy. Just a little drag," James instructed.

His coughing stopped, John forced a smile. He waved the pipe in his hand. "I don't know if I should do this. My mother might not want me to smoke."

"She is not here," James said. "You're a soldier now."

"That I am." He took several puffs on James's pipe. "It does make you feel different." He exhaled the smoke. After a few more attempts at smoking John said, "I don't feel so good." He handed the pipe back to James. "I'm going to be sick." He got up from the log and ran behind the tent.

James heard him throwing up. "Sorry, John," he said.

After a few minutes, John slowly walked back and slumped down on the log near James. "That was awful," John told him. "I'm never going to smoke. My mouth tastes like swill. I feel just awful. How can you do it?"

"I'm sorry, I didn't think you would be sick. You do look as green as grass."

John sighed loudly. "I'm never going to smoke. Never. There is nothing comforting about smoking. How can you enjoy smoking?"

"Aw," answered James, "I'm used to it."

Just then John's father walked up with Alexander. "You need to inform the soldiers to douse their fires."

"What's the matter with you? Are you sick, John?" asked his brother.

"I'm all right," replied John.

James laughed. "He tried smoking my pipe."

Mr. Montgomery tried to hide a smile. "Didn't you like smoking, John?"

"No, I did not, and I am never going to put a pipe in my mouth ever again."

John took his fife from his case and said to James, "Get your drum, we have work to do." He coughed and felt like his insides were burning up but John Montgomery knew his duty and he put his fife to his mouth.

"Ready?" asked James as he twirled his drumsticks.

John nodded. He was always ready to serve his country. They drummed and blew orders to the soldiers. It was time to rest before the next day came.

The next morning they broke camp and the long march to the fort was almost over. The soldiers had their tumpline on their backs, their haversacks over their shoulders, and their muskets ready. The wagons were loaded. The soldiers marched until the sun was high in the sky. John didn't want to complain but his feet hurt, his mouth was tired from playing the fife, and his fingers were tired, too. He was grateful when told by the lieutenant that they would stop and rest. John just wanted to drink some water and take off his boots. He had been warned that if his feet had swelled, he would not be able to get his boots back on. He sat on the ground and was grateful to rest. He laid his tricorn hat beside him.

Private Campbell walked over with a bucket of water and the dipper. "Here fifer, have a drink and be sure to fill your water canteen."

John took the dipper gratefully and slowly drank the cool water. "Thanks," he said as the water cooled his parched throat. He put the dipper back in the bucket and lay down on the cool green weeds that lined the road. He used his tumpline as a pillow. After laying there for a few minutes he knew he would fall asleep. He made himself sit up; sleep would come tonight after the marching army reached Moore's Fort.

James was beside him and had fallen asleep the minute he lay on the ground. His drum was by his head but he still had his drumsticks in his hands. John punched him in the side with his elbow. "James, wake up, they are passing out water."

James opened his eyes, moaned, and said, "I've got water. I didn't know how tired I could be." Both boys forgot they often walked many miles working in their father's fields in the hot sun. But this was marching and after a few miles, marching was not enjoyable.

In a few minutes, John picked up his fife, wiped it off, and was ready to play. "Get up James, we've got to be in front."

James struggled to his feet, picked up his drum, and twirled his drumsticks. "Ready?"

The sounds of the fife and the drumbeats began, and the soldiers with their rifles and muskets got into line. The notes played the marching rhythm and the soldiers trudged on. In a few hours Moore's Fort came into view. It was a welcome sight. Captain Dasey was leading the men in front. He looked at John and smiled. "The fort," he said and pointed ahead. The long march was over.

CHAPTER 9

"*General Greene said* that even though we left the Guilford Courthouse in defeat we did a lot of damage to Cornwallis. He lost a lot of men and has a lot of wounded. The General does not see how the British can withstand another battle." Sergeant Porter spoke to the men in a quiet voice. The sergeant and the soldiers were tired from their march to Moore's Fort. He wanted to say something positive to help the men. "The Scotch-Irish fought bravely with their fine and accurate shooting. We are grateful for those volunteers who help us when we need it most." He smiled and waited for comments.

"Hear, hear," the men said as they sat around on their tumplines or leaned against the wall.

General Greene joined them. He was tall in stature and wore a clean uniform. "Men," he began, "our spies tell me that Cornwallis has left Guilford Courthouse and has begun to march north. His army is crippled and I don't see how he can win many more battles. We are to wait here until we get further orders from General George Washington." He smiled broadly. "The Guilford Courthouse battle was a battle fought bravely by all of you. The wounded are being cared for by the doctor. And now we rest and wait." General Greene nodded then turned and walked back to his office in the fort.

"The General has also ordered extra rations for us. You will receive one extra gill of beans, butter, and half a pound of beef. There will also be one egg per man for breakfast tomorrow. And if some volunteers will go fishing we will have fish, too," the sergeant concluded. The men let out a loud cheer. They had known hunger when fighting.

"I'll go fish," volunteered John.

"Me too," said Alex. Others volunteered and off they went with poles to the river.

It was quiet at the river and hot even for March. The boys found a spot in the shade and put worms on their hooks. Their corks bobbed in the water. They were quiet because they did not want to scare the fish. After a while Alex whispered, "The fish do not seem to be biting."

"Be patient."

They heard some shouting and looked up to see a soldier with a fish on his line.

"Well, someone is lucky. But one fish will not feed this army."

"Remember in the Bible the story about the fish?"

"Of course, I remember." Suddenly Alex felt a pull on his line and his cork was pulled under the water. "John, I've got a bite!"

"Careful, bring it in gently, don't want to lose him. I'll help." John stood up and grabbed his net to put it under the fish. "It's a big one!"

Alex grabbed the fish with his hands. "It's a nice striped bass. Must weigh two or three pounds."

"It's a big one all right," agreed John.

Alex unhooked the fish, put another hook and line in it, and put it back in the water.

"Looks like we will have fish tonight," he said proudly. As he reached for his pole he felt pain in his shoulder. He grimaced.

"Are you all right, Alex?" asked John.

"Yes, my shoulder hurts when I move sometimes. I forget and use it."

"Do you need to see the doctor?"

"The doctor has enough serious injuries to look after."

"Are you keeping it clean like the doctor said?"

"Yes, of course. Dr. Rush said it was important to keep all wounds clean. The application of the comfrey leaves helped heal up my shoulder."

"But you must be careful. Don't do anything that will cause you to open the wound," John cautioned.

"I won't."

They were sitting quietly again when John felt a pull on his line. "I've got a bite." His cork disappeared in the water. John pulled his line out of the water and sure enough there was a big bass. John smiled broadly as he attached the fish to the line with Alex's fish. The fish flapped their tails in the water. The creek water was cool to John's hands, and he left them in the water for a few seconds before he put a worm on his hook and put his pole in again.

The two boys fished all afternoon and caught a few more fish. They often heard shouts from the others when they caught a fish. John and Alex were quiet because their father had taught them that shouting would scare the fish away. When everyone went back to the fort there was enough fish for each soldier. With their extra rations and some bread the soldiers would not be hungry. Fish were frying in every pan and the corporal took out his harmonica and played for the men as they gathered around their campfires.

CHAPTER 10

The days passed quietly at the fort. John was needed as a fifer at dawn and in the evening. A few troops went out almost every day to check on Indian skirmishes, but most days were peaceful. Early one morning after a rider arrived at the fort and asked to see General Greene, John and James had to play assembly. When the soldiers were assembled and at attention, General Greene spoke. "Cornwallis has surrendered at Yorktown. Well, he didn't surrender but sent his lieutenant to General Washington to do it for him." The men who had been standing quietly let out a loud cheer. James played a drum roll and John joined in with his fife.

"I am certain the British will be leaving our country as soon as they can." Another loud cheer came from the men standing in front of him. "Now we celebrate the Yorktown victory. I have requested that fish house punch be made; it is General Washington's favorite drink and it is good. You are all invited inside for some good cheer and fish house punch in honor of our good General Washington. Dismissed."

John ran to his brother. "I hope this means that we can go home now."

Alex smiled wistfully, "We have to stay until our time is up; it's just a few more weeks. Remember, we signed up for five years."

"I didn't know how long five years was."

"Neither did I." Alexander put his hand on his brother's shoulder. "You are as tall as I am."

John smiled, "Am I?" Alexander nodded. They walked together and sat in the shade.

"These next weeks will be very long, won't they?" John asked.

His brother nodded in agreement. John sighed. They went inside. John and Alexander stood in the room with all the soldiers. There was much laughing and cheering as the men were given punch. It wasn't often that they had reason to celebrate, and the soldiers were enjoying themselves. When it came time for John and his brother to get their cups filled with fish house punch, Sergeant Porter asked, "Wouldn't you boys rather have beer or cider? This punch has Jamaican rum, cognac, peach brandy, and lemon juice in it. I can dilute it with some tea, but I don't think you should drink this punch without the tea. I just want to caution you that it is powerful and strong."

"We can handle it, Sergeant Porter. I'm now eighteen, and Alexander is twenty."

"All right, but it's against my better judgment." He dipped into the punch and gave each boy a large helping of punch. John gulped his drink. He turned red in the face and tried to talk, but couldn't. "Ah-ah-ah—this isn't like the punch our mother makes at all!" He put his cup down on the table.

"John," Alex said patting him on the back, "don't drink so fast." Alex raised his cup to his lips and sipped.

"You won't like it," said John as Alex kept sipping his drink.

Alex made a face. "No, I don't like it much. But I suppose a soldier should be able to drink it if General Washington does."

Smiling, Sergeant Porter said, "Tell you what boys, I'll just put a little tea in your cups and no one will know that you're not drinking the real thing. That's the way I like this punch—with a little tea mixed with it."

John and Alex looked at the stocky sergeant. "If that is the way you think the punch is best, then that is the way we will have it too," Alex said quietly.

Sergeant Porter poured some tea into their cups without any of the other soldiers seeing him. "I think you will like it this way best."

"You are correct, Sergeant Porter, and thank you." The two brothers nodded to their sergeant and went to find James.

"James," called John, "how do you like this fish house punch?"

"I don't, I'm having cider. I love cider." He smiled. "We will soon be going home, John. I am going to miss you. When I go home I will have to help my father get the crops planted. After that I hope I can ride over to see both you and Alex."

"Oh, that would be fine."

"I've got twin sisters; both of them have flaming red hair just like mine. I may have to bring them as we have grandparents not far from your house. Maybe my whole family could come."

"My family likes company, James." John turned to Alex. "Our parents would like to meet your sisters. Are they pretty?"

With a big smile on his face, James nodded. "Yes." Alex and John smiled back.

John saw the corporal get out his harmonica. "Come on, let's join in the singing." The three young men stood together and began to sing *The Freedom Song* with their fellow soldiers.

As the days went by, John hid the fact that he was lonesome for home; he suspected that his brother was too. But neither one said anything about home. They fulfilled their duties at the fort, but each day brought more longing to go home. They began to wonder what their father and mother were doing. Their father would be working in the fields. Michael was now old enough to help him. Their mother, they knew, was busy cooking and washing and keeping the house clean. How they longed to sit at the table and eat with the family. The days seemed to pass very slowly, but finally their time was up and they could go home.

Early one morning Sergeant Porter came to them and said, "Alex and John, your time is up. You can go home. You have fulfilled your duties and now you may leave."

Being good soldiers they said, "Fine, Sergeant." When the sergeant walked away they hugged each other and smiled broadly. They were jumping for joy when he turned around and watched them. "I will be leaving early in the morning to go home, too. I am now Mr. Porter. If you want, I can give you a ride as I will be passing your homestead on my way. Of you can walk home if you—"

John interrupted, "Oh no, we would appreciate a ride, Mr. Porter."

Alex said anxiously, "We would rather ride than walk, sir—er, Mr. Porter. I have had enough of marching and walking." John gave a sigh of relief. He had had plenty of marching, too.

The next morning at sunrise, John and Alex threw their haversacks in the back of the wagon and jumped on the wagon seat beside Mr. Porter. They had said their good-byes to the friends they had made. Sergeant Ross opened the gate for them and waved them on their way, the wagon rattling and slowly moving away from the fort. The two brothers had happy smiles on their faces as the fort faded in the distance and the wagon headed in the direction of home.

"I wondered if I would ever see home again. It has been such a long time. When we signed up for five years, I don't think we realized how long that would be," sighed Alex.

"I know I didn't," John told him. "But I am glad I did. The war was hard, but the British will go back to England."

"Good riddance," stated Mr. Porter. "Now boys, when you get hungry, I've got corn cakes and some bread and cheese in the back of the wagon."

"Thank you, Mr. Porter, but I'm too excited to eat. I can't wait to get home," Alex said.

"I'm excited too. I can't wait. Our Mother and Father and Michael will be glad to see us, but not as glad as I will be to see them." There was joy in John's voice as he spoke.

"We just learned that we have a new brother named Philip we have never seen," Alex volunteered.

"Well, well, well, that's nice. Lots of surprises for you boys," Mr. Porter said, pulling on the horses' reins.

The three bounced along in the wagon and were silent, each with his own thoughts. The creaking of the wagon and the occasional bird song were the only sounds to be heard. The trees and grasses beside the road were lush and green; the sign of recent rains. Soon Mr. Porter shaded his face with his hand. "I believe it is about two o'clock by the sun. And here we are ready to turn toward your house, down this lane."

"Mr. Porter, please let us out. I would like to get out and walk home from here." John turned to Alex, "Is that all right, Alex?"

"Yes, let's do that. I can smell the earth from the freshly planted soil. What a happy day this is! We're almost home!"

"All right, boys." Mr. Porter called "Whoa," pulled hard on the reins, and stopped the horses.

John and Alex grabbed their belongings and jumped down from the wagon. John's hat fell off and he bent down to pick it up. He brushed the dirt from his hat and sat it back on his head. Squinting into the sun, he looked at Mr. Porter, "Thank you sir, for the ride."

"You're welcome, soldiers."

"Thank you, Mr. Porter," said Alex, "but we are soldiers no more." He smiled. "Good-bye."

Mr. Porter waved good-bye, "Giddy up," he spoke to the horses, and the wagon began to move slowly. He flicked the reins. "Giddy up," he repeated, and the wagon moved faster. John and Alex waved to him and then began walking fast down the lane.

"We're almost home."

"John, we are home. We're walking on Montgomery land right now."

"We are, aren't we?" John jumped, gave a shout, and started running, with Alex close behind him.

Their house came into view. They saw the large poplar tree in the yard, their father's chair on the porch, washing on the clothesline, the sheets blowing in the wind. It was if they had never been away. Suddenly, their mother ran out the door, down the porch steps, and into the lane. She held up her calico dress so she could run.

"Alex, John, you're here. My brave boys! Welcome home!" Tears were running down her face as she smiled. She grabbed both of them and gave them both a big hug. "I prayed you would come home safely."

"Oh, Mother," Alex tried to talk, but tears sprang to his eyes. "Mother, you're crying. Don't be sad."

She laughed, "I'm not sad, I'm so happy you're home that I'm crying and laughing at the same time." She looked at both of them. "How you have grown; you're both so tall and handsome!"

John grinned and picked up his mother and began swinging her around. "I'm home," he cried, "I'm home!"

EPILOGUE

This is a work of historical fiction; however, the Montgomery family is real. John and his brother enlisted in the Revolutionary War when John was thirteen and Alexander was fifteen for five years of service. They left the army in June of 1782.

A few years later, John married Susannah Elizabeth Porter and they had eight children. Two years after Susannah's death in 1802, he married Elizabeth Harris. They had four children, but only one daughter, Sarah, survived. John's daughter, Martha May, married the author's great-great-grandfather.

In 1779, John became a lieutenant in the Second Battalion, 72nd Regiment of the Virginia Militia.

John eventually moved with his family to Peoria, Illinois, where he lived until he died at the age of seventy-nine. He is buried in Princeville Cemetery.